Hibs Boy

The Life and Violent Times of Scotland's Most Notorious Football Hooligan

Hibs Boy

The Life and Violent Times of Scotland's
Most Notorious Football Hooligan

Andy Blance

Fort Publishing Ltd

First published in 2009 by Fort Publishing Ltd, Old Belmont House,
12 Robsland Avenue, Ayr, KA7 2RW

© Andy Blance 2009

All rights reserved. No part of this publication may be reproduced, stored in a retrieval system, or transmitted, in any form or by any means, electronic, mechanical, photocopying, recording or otherwise, without the prior permission of the publishers and copyright holders.

Andy Blance has asserted his rights under the Copyright, Designs and Patents Act, 1988 to be recognised as the author of this work.

Printed by Bell and Bain Ltd, Glasgow

Cover photograph by Dougie Thomson: www.dougiethomson.com

Typeset by 3btype.com

Graphic design by Mark Blackadder

ISBN: 978-1-905769-15-5

CONTENTS

Foreword by Irvine Welsh — 7
Acknowledgements — 13
They Said It . . . — 15

1	Early Days	21
2	The Skinhead Years	33
3	A Legend Is Born	41
4	Why We Fight	48
5	Love and Marriage	53
6	When One Door Closes . . .	58
7	Aberdeen: Just a Good Honest Mob	65
8	The Kronk: the Road to War	74
9	The Kronk: the Attack	83
10	The Kronk: Paying the Price	89
11	Hearts: Chasing the Scum	99
12	Doing Time	110
13	Rangers: In the Belly of the Beast	119
14	Edinburgh Days, Edinburgh Nights	130
15	Celtic: the Day of Reckoning	141
16	A Nice Little Earner	148
17	Scotland's Other Mobs	159
18	England's Finest	172
19	The Auld Enemy	184
20	Battles in Brussels	192
21	A Mini Mafia	197
22	All Things Must Pass	203
23	Rolling Back the Years	208
24	Regrets? I Have a Few	213

Men of the CCS — 219

FOREWORD

Irvine Welsh

It was around 1984 when I first became aware of the growth of the casual movement in Edinburgh. I'd been living mostly in London since 1978, but still came up to my home town on a regular basis for Hibs games. The Whelahan bus, run by my friend, Scott Bootland, contained a motley crew of 1970s Hibs hooligans, northern soul freaks, punks, mods, piss-heads, drug-fiends and other misfits. We weren't affiliated to the official supporters associations, thus the Whelahan was one of the few buses that let on so-called 'casuals'; boys around 14–17 years of age, many of whom were younger relatives and friends of the Whelahan regulars. (Another bus with an open-door policy towards the emerging teenage mob was the Liberton branch, which Andy Blance and his mates regularly travelled on.)

A lot of the older lads in their twenties and thirties disdained these teenagers, with their strange clothes, lack of scarfs etc, but although I was ten years too old and way too badly dressed to be a casual, I recall being quite impressed at the time. I thought they had a bit of sartorial style (when I thought about Mickey McMillan's green site helmet and gold Doc Martens in the early seventies) and that they all seemed pretty tight with each other.

It was easy to understand the reticence of the old guard. Hooliganism in the seventies was a very different phenomenon to its 1980s incarnation. It was possible back then to indulge in aggressive activity at football, without necessarily being labelled a hooligan. Football terraces back then were noisy, colourful theatres, and you could choose to be centre stage or elect to wait in the wings. In other words, it was a type of behaviour that one could flit in and out of, rather than the determined lifestyle it would later become.

Also, in the seventies, the street-gang culture was the dominant force in Edinburgh. You had the Leith Team, Niddrie Terror, Mental Drylaw, Lochend Shamrock, Pilton Derry, Inch Cumbie etc etc, all prefixed with a youthful 'Y'. (My personal favourite moniker of the time was Y-MASS – the Young Mental Amsterdam Shotgun Squad.) This meant that apart from the Edinburgh derby against Hearts, and the visit of the Glasgow clubs, aggro at Easter Road was quite often between Hibs boys from different parts of the city.

The away games tended to promote more solidarity, and this was how many people got involved in hooliganism in the seventies, simply through being a travelling fan. For me it was as mundane as having a preference for the train as I got car and bus sick as a kid. But this mode of travel meant having to navigate the inevitable reception committees of would-be ambushers on the walk from the station to the ground. So it made sense to stick together, with other young Hibs fans. You initially attended these fixtures with friends from your own area or your local school, but soon made pals from other parts of the town; in my case, Mickey and Kenny McMillan and Bob Carlin from Niddrie, John Boyle, Jimmy Lugton, Jimmy Crawford and Deano Rafferty from the South Side, George Shipton and James 'Scrap' Ferguson from Tollcross.

In the seventies, the media hadn't got a proper handle on hooliganism to any great extent. As it changed and developed, it took them a very, very long time to come anywhere near understanding the phenomenon. The first chant I heard referencing it at Easter Road was 'hooly-hooly-hooly-gans'; a largely disapproving cry, almost pointing out troublemakers, and even when this morphed into a prouder statement with songs like 'Eddie Turnbull's Soccer Hooligans' there was still an ironic, tongue-in-cheek aspect to it all.

Throughout the seventies at Easter Road, despite the odd notable battles on the way to the ground, the hooligan scene inside the stadium exponentially declined. This was mainly to do with putting seats in the 'Cave' or Cowshed (the covered terracing where the Famous Five now stands), killing much of the atmosphere at the ground. The more vocal Hibs fans used to congregate here in the sixties, but it became the centre of trouble with missiles coming onto the pitch from this tightly packed area, and clubs who brought a big travelling support (Hearts, Rangers, Celtic) would try and 'take' this end. Back then, there was a drive to shut down or nullify problem areas of terracing. Brian Clough once famously threatened to shut the Trent End at Nottingham Forest.

Emasculating the Cave by transforming it into what was the dreariest seating area in the history of the game was a big blow, as it dispersed the home singing support (and hoolie element within it) onto the inhospitable slopes of Shaw Heights, the huge, open main terracing. Though some of the more raucous elements decanted to the North Enclosure, the atmosphere didn't pick up inside the stadium till Shaw Heights was levelled and covered, forming the East Terracing which still exists today, augmented with bucket seats.

This lack of atmosphere was compounded by the railed sectioning of the ground, which meant rival supporters could no longer change ends at half-time. Then, following Hillsbourgh in 1997 and the Taylor report, and the riot at the 1980 Scottish Cup final, the immediate segregation of rival supporters was enforced and a timetable for all-seater stadiums was established. This had the effect of changing the nature of hooliganism; the big rows now happened almost exclusively outside the stadiums.

It changed the hooligan too. There was always a largely performative element to seventies thuggery, with its taunting and occasionally charging across the 'no man's land' between rival fans and spilling onto the pitch. However, with the numbers involved (due to the mixing of drunks, singers, kids looking for excitement with genuine hoolies) it could be a lot more dangerous for bystanders. But the changes in fan organisation, policing and stadia meant that hooliganism became a more serious activity for the participants. Some thought had to go into the row; you couldn't simply just show up at the ground and expect it to go off. While these developments made life safer for the so-called average fan, it became increasingly more dangerous for the hooligan, who now had to be a serious street-savvy player, rather than a dilettante just coming along for the laugh.

One thing that struck me as being different at the games I attended in London was that generational gap in hooliganism at Hibs. Down there, the old school thugs tended to stick with it, while the 70s hooligans at Easter Road saw it being a largely teenage thing, and tended to disdain it as they moved into their mid-twenties. A lot of this was undoubtedly to do with the impact of the street gangs as the main focus of thug loyalty; fighting on a Friday night with your mates in Rose Street against boys from another scheme was more acceptable than fighting on a Saturday afternoon against boys from another city. This changed with the new breed of Hibs hoolie (as they were back then in the mid-eighties), who were a tight, well-togged mob, drawing boys from all over the city and beyond. For the first time ever, Edinburgh had one, big, united 'firm'. This basically is where Andy Blance and the CCS come in.

A lot of fisherman's tales abound about 500 or 1,000 a side, but it's been my experience on both sides of the border that there's a lot of theatrics and bravado around the hoolie scene. Even at its height, irrespective of the total numbers involved, you basically had the same bunch of game scrappers, no more than two dozen a side, sometimes only half-a-dozen (streets and people are only so wide), who went at it with ruthless dedication, while we lesser mortals gesticulated from behind barriers, charged and retreated, or peeled off to 'windmill' with some other unskilled mug. Television footage on hooliganism invariably shows police focusing on those colourful, lumbering amateurs who throw plastic folding chairs at each other across squares, rather than the top boys going at it toe-to-toe.

Blance was one of those top boys at Hibs, and over a number of seasons. He gained national and local media notoriety and was under active surveillance by police units for years. So his credentials in telling this story are impeccable. Over the years, I've got to know many of the boys from that era, and some of them are close friends. I've seen it all kick off with them at Ibrox, Pittodrie, Anderlecht and numerous other places, including the unlikely venue of Ingliston Show Grounds at a Madness concert. My personal view on the 'Hibs casuals' was that they were a phenomenon of their times, and that if you were going to have a mob (and every club, to a greater or lesser extent, did back in the eighties and early nineties) then it was better to have an effective one. Many non-hooligan Hibs fans attest that as the reputation of the thug element spread, it made them less likely to be attacked on visits to places like Ibrox. The CCS certainly earned many plaudits for their exploits. West Ham's notorious ICF were even once moved, after hearing of the CCS performance at an away 'friendly' at deadly rivals Millwall, to place an advert in the *Evening Standard* congratulating them 'on a job well done'.

I got to know Andy Blance through a mutual friend from Leith. While he looks like he's from central hoolie casting with his shaved head, tatts and stocky scrapper's build, the stereotype is quickly dispelled in conversation as an erudite and thoughtful man soon emerges. Unlike many of the boys I've got to know over the years (some as much through music and the club scene as the football) Andy isn't a big party animal (he's teetotal) and is now very much a family man. He still follows his team, but like many of the lads from that era, is more likely to be sitting in the good seats with his son or father, than swapping tales of bygone days with former faces. That sense of perspective helps inform this book.

There will obviously be people who think that such things are better not discussed, perhaps that they are an affront to a game which they profess to love. However, 'the game' has long since sold its soul to commerce, to the point that we have a scenario where one player is to be transferred for over £100 million. That money could open a new state-of-the-art school in a UK city, and give five hundred kids per year a better start in life. Alongside this kind of ongoing obscenity, a bunch of young men deciding they want to get together for a row on a Saturday seems a very minor issue.

It's also important to remember that when the CCS were kicking off back in the Eighties, unemployment had trebled from 1.2 million in 1979 to 3.6 million in 1983, and Edinburgh had become the AIDS capital of Europe. At this grim point in our social history, many young men with time on their hands and little opportunity in employment, were succumbing to the nightmare of heroin addiction. At the same time Hibs casuals were fostering a sense of pride, belonging and community amongst their members, which meant that very few (if any) of them were tempted to take that route.

It would be erroneous and ridiculous to see the CCS as some kind of DIY Boy Scouts or BBs, but they are part of a long-standing and ubiquitous tradition. You still hear the old boys in the pubs on Leith Walk and Gorgie Road reminiscing about the Ted mobs of the fifties, such as the Jubilee and Valder gangs, which were often based around local cafes. You also hear of the chaps from the sixties and seventies talking about the 'young mental' street gangs of that era. In all those cases there was plenty of violence, though this is now often put aside in the nostalgic afterglow. That's because the sense of belonging that pervaded those scenes remains the predominant memory of the participants, after the hormones and restlessness of youth's yesteryear have long been spent. Despite their continuing demonisation and the hysteria that still surrounds this issue, the Hibs casuals of the eighties and nineties are no different. This is their story.

Irvine Welsh
March 2009.

ACKNOWLEDGEMENTS

Thanks to everyone who supplied information and provided quotes. I am especially grateful to those friends who dug out old photos, especially Davie Ritchie, Tattie, Dykes, Dougie Duffy, Greedy and John McGeever. I must also record my thanks to Dougie 'Greengrass' Thomson for the excellent cover photograph and to the boys who posed for him (from left to right they are: Neil, Kev, Tattie, Mikey, Taylor, Blair, Girvan, Bongo, Bri Mac, Tooly, Keith, Johnny, Paul and Jamie).

Beefy came up with the idea for the CCS flag in the background. Thanks big man and sorry you couldn't make it for the photo. But I know fishing comes before everything else these days! Well done to Ricky Ragina for supplying the Hibs fixture lists, which proved very useful.

My dad, my brother Chris and my sisters Michele and Sally-Ann put up with a lot from me when we were growing up. You stuck by me and I am grateful.

Thanks also to James McCarroll of Fort Publishing for his faith in the book and to Chris Terry for his assistance with the technical side and the writing. I must also express my gratitude to my lawyer, Stephen Morrison, for looking after me so well for years and for 'legalling' the book.

I will always be grateful to Irvine Welsh for agreeing to write the Foreword. He is a true Hibby, a great novelist and a real party animal.

Sorry if I've missed anyone. You were all so important to me. You gave me times I will never forget. Thanks to one and all.

Finally, I have to thank my girlfriend, Kim, and my sons Kevin, Jamie and Jack for neglecting them while I was writing this book. I promise to make it up to you.

CCS R.I.P.

Horan, Ben, Stu Douglas, Davie Happel, Terry 'Tel Boy' Reilly, Ian 'Dodgy' Donald, Dino Cozzi, Mow, Worzel, Andy Parker, Chris McCaw, Moysey, Paul Black, David Keddie.
God bless you all.

Andy Blance, *Inverkeithing*
August 2009

THEY SAID IT . . .

About Andy Blance

'The axeman boss of Hibees casuals.'
Daily Record, 5 May 2003

'One of the top boys, a leader of the CCS.'
Scotland on Sunday, 11 November 1990

'A hard man in every sense of the word. A real character. He was instrumental in the organisation of the CCS.'
Graham Walker, administrator, www.hibs.net

'The CCS is a religion. Andy Blance is its high priest.'
Cazshie, CCS member

'When I first met him I didn't believe it was him. I had heard so many stories about this violent, out-of-control, wild man. I couldn't believe how polite and well-mannered he was.'
Alex McAulay, security-company owner and Blance's former employer

'Andy Blance has devoted most of his adult life to football hooliganism. [He] is an axe-wielding football hooligan, once convicted of attempted murder.'
Sunday Times, 9 June 1996

'He is like a brother to me'
Bongo, former CCS member

'[His] behaviour could not be tolerated in a civilised society.'
Lord Kirkwood, sentencing Blance to five years in prison at the High Court in 1991

'He is right beside your shoulder at all times. He would never run away and leave his mates.'
James Girvan, CCS member

'The leader of one of Scotland's most notorious casual gangs.'
Daily Record, 5 May 2003

'I was young and impressionable. He was someone you looked up to. He had guts; he was the man.'
Fraser, former CCS member

'A good friend made CCS style.'
Taylor, CCS member

'Andy is a very pleasant person when I'm in his company. I know he has a bad reputation. But he is a Hibs supporter and very proud and passionate about his club.'
Frank Dougan, Treasurer, Hibernian Supporters Association

'He is a real Arthur Daley, a wide boy. But he was always first into a fight. He was a game guy.'
Tattie, former CCS member

'When the shit hits the fan he is totally reliable.'
Mikey Neri, CCS member

'Is he Scotland's most dedicated hooligan? I don't know, but he's certainly up there.'
Member of Rangers Inter City Firm

THEY SAID IT...

'Despite his image Andy is much more than a thug. He is a highly intelligent man with a great sense of humour. He is a great mate to have and he would do anything for you.'

Cazshie

'While he looks like he's from central hoolie casting with his shaved head, tatts and stocky scrapper's build the stereotype is quickly dispelled in conversation as an erudite and thoughtful man soon emerges.'

Irvine Welsh, novelist

About the Capital City Service

'These people are animals. They are not real fans and we want nothing to do with them.'

Douglas Cromb, former Hibs chairman, quoted in the *Daily Record*

'We were like a family. You fuck with one Hibs boy you fuck with us all.'

James Girvan

'Hibs casuals have turned parts of Edinburgh's city centre into a weekend war zone and have been implicated in protection rackets, drug rings and criminal damage.'

Stuart Cosgrove, in *Hampden Babylon* (Edinburgh 1991)

'The battles with Hibs are legend. It was always a fucking mental place to go.'

Dan Rivers, in *Congratulations: You Have Just Met the Casuals* (London 2005)

'Hibs since the casual scene started in Scotland have given us the most grief.'

Davey Carrick, in *Rangers ICF* (London 2008)

'Hibs by this time had established themselves as the mob everyone wanted to turn over. They were widely regarded as the top firm in Scotland.'

John O'Kane, in *Celtic Soccer Crew* (London 2006)

'Millwall supporters have had a bad name over the years but this is the worst I've seen and I've been here for twenty-four years.'
Greig Tarrant, landlord of a Millwall pub, after a 'visit' by the CCS, quoted in *Edinburgh Evening News*, 13 October 1990

'A few cars with their windows smashed, some riotous behaviour in pubs and restaurants, a few dozen arrests and some stabbings. And that was just the Hibs fans.'

The Herald, 5 October 1992: reporting on trouble in Brussels before the Anderlecht–Hibs UEFA Cup tie.

'The most feared soccer firm in Scotland . . . between 1988 and 1994 the Capital City Service (CCS) dominated Scottish hooliganism.'
Nick Lowles and Andy Nicholls, in *The A–L of Britain's Football Hooligan Gangs* (London 2007)

'The Capital City Service remains the most active group of casuals in the Edinburgh area and they appear to be run on a territorial basis but under one gang structure.'
Lothian and Borders Police, Special Bulletin, 15 August 1989

'You certainly couldn't wear your colours to certain grounds in the West of Scotland. Now ordinary fans can wear scarves at games and that is in large part due to the CCS.'

Frank Dougan

THEY SAID IT . . .

'In several instances I was happy they were there, particularly when we travelled to Glasgow. The casuals are part of Scottish football history. There is even a display about them in the Scottish football museum at Hampden.'

Graham Walker

'Before the CCS, Hibs buses got tanned. Scarfers had to take their scarves off. We changed all that. They never thanked us for it but life became much easier for them.'

Mikey Neri

'A lot of scarfers were grateful to the CCS. Before us they got spanked by Celtic and Rangers. They came through in their hordes, sat on the pavements and took over. They really took the piss. When we got organised all that changed. Easter Road became a fortress.'

Fraser

'At first they [scarfers] liked the CCS because they were no longer getting attacked everywhere they went. Their principles have changed. They have forgotten what scarfers had to go through before the advent of the casuals. They are ungrateful. Without the CCS they would have got a lot more beatings.'

Bongo

'I loved every minute of it. I loved being involved. I still really miss it. I think about it every day. I lived for a Saturday.'

Tattie

'No regrets. That's what we did. If I was twenty years younger I would do it all over again. I made a lot of good friends and I have great memories.'

Fraser

'I don't regret it. I learnt a lot and became a better person for it. I enjoyed the awaydays, the laughs and giggles.'

Bongo

'I don't look back on it with pride but it did mould me into the person I am now. It gave me a sense of belonging, a feeling of being part of something bigger than myself. It made me more self-confident. Being Hibs boys we felt we were a match for anyone.'

Cazshie

'It was a change in my life for the better. I made so many good friends.'

Taylor

1
EARLY DAYS

Those close to me have always maintained that my personality changed forever when my parents split up. I was six at the time and I suppose it must have affected me. The question is: did it push me over the edge? Was it responsible for a life characterised by criminality and violence? It is a statistical fact that children whose parents split up are more likely to get into trouble, so that might explain my behaviour over the past thirty-odd years. On the other hand my siblings – one brother, two sisters – did not go down the same road. Although none of them were angels they eventually became upstanding citizens. Maybe being the oldest child made the loss of my mother more difficult to take. Were my brothers and sisters just too young to know what was going on and therefore less traumatised?

I honestly don't know the answers.

I am sure that neither of my parents would have thought for one minute that I would turn out the way I did when I was born in the Edinburgh suburb of Corstorphine in 1965. It is a quiet, middle-class area to the west of the city, a place where teachers, accountants and bank managers live. My father was a white-collar civil servant in what would now be the Ministry of Defence. He was, and is, a respectable, hard-working man, someone you could trust, a man who kept his nose clean and put his family first. My mother – who hailed from London – also came from a good family.

When I was still a toddler dad got a posting to the Royal dockyard in Rosyth, which is in Fife. Rosyth is about ten miles from Edinburgh

– on the north side of the Firth of Forth, barely a stone's throw from the Forth Road Bridge – and we moved to a house there so that dad could be closer to his office. By this time my brother and older sister had been born and they would soon be followed by a second sister. With a new career, a nice house and a growing family dad must have felt on top of the world. It is amazing how quickly things can change, how your whole life can be thrown into turmoil overnight.

The split with my mum hit him hard. They had produced four children within the space of six years, which indicates that the marriage was, at least initially, a happy one. I have no idea why they broke up. All I know is that my mother left the family home, then came back briefly, then left again, this time for good. The tension and emotional distress must have been unbearable and even at such a tender age I am sure my siblings and I must have been aware of it.

As a lone parent a huge burden fell on dad's shoulders. He now had four young children to bring up on his own. Many men would have packed in work and lived on state benefits but he didn't entertain that thought for a second, even if in financial terms he might not have been that much worse off. Working for a living, earning your keep, standing on your own two feet; these principles have always been important to him and he did his best to impart them to us as well. So he continued to work full time and when he came home at night he got stuck into the washing, cooking and cleaning. There was some assistance from outside: a home help provided by the social-work department came in at half-past three to look after us until dad got back from his office at half-five and my great aunt Ella, who lived close by, also helped out. Nevertheless dad was on the go virtually round the clock.

For the most part it must have been a relentless and exhausting way of life. It was also very difficult for him in financial terms. Money was always in short supply and our single-income status meant we occasionally qualified for free school meals. His only luxury, if you could call it that, was table tennis; he played once a week and reached a high standard, winning medals and cups and even represented Scotland.

Despite the many problems we faced as a family it was always a happy home, full of life and laughter. There were four boys next door, who were around the same age as us, and we all played happily together, no doubt annoying the older neighbours with our games and pranks, which seemed to go on from first light until darkness fell. It was also at this time I was introduced to the institution that has become the defining passion of my life: Hibernian Football Club. Although I was inept as a player I was an enthusiastic spectator from the word go, attracted by the sights and sounds and colours that surrounded the professional game. My earliest football memories are of my dad and my 'uncle' taking me to matches. One week we went to Easter Road, the next to Tynecastle, until I was old enough to realise that you don't support two teams especially when they are such bitter rivals. I hate to admit it but I must have attended quite a few Hearts games before I saw the light. But why did I choose Hibs? Probably on the same basis that boys across the world choose their club: they want to follow the same team as their dads. One day, I asked him:

'Dad, who do you support?'

'Hibs,' he replied.

That was good enough for me. From that moment on I was a Hibby and soon I was following the team home and away. I travelled all over Scotland to watch Hibs, usually by train, and I would be well looked after by two older Fife boys: Craig from Lochgelly and Bernie from Cowdenbeath. Over the years I came to the conclusion that supporting Hibs ran in the Blance family; that it was in our DNA. It was only when this book was being written that I discovered the real reason my dad followed them. It was because his dad, my grandfather, had been a Jambo! Dad had chosen Hibs just to annoy his father, who, I am led to believe, was something of a disciplinarian. I am still coming to terms with the knowledge that a close blood relative followed the Scum!

To get the money for these trips to watch Hibs I took on a variety of odd jobs: a paper round, cutting the neighbours' grass, taking empty lemonade bottles back for the deposits. Despite my notoriety I have always had a nose for business – many in the CCS call me Arthur Daley or Del Boy – and this may have been how it started.

In other areas of my life things were not quite so harmonious. My first criminal act had been perpetrated at age four, when I was caught shoplifting from Rosyth Co-op. It was before my parents went their separate ways, which makes me slightly sceptical about the theory that the breakdown in their relationship was the cause of my delinquency. What is indisputable is that from then on 'trouble' became my middle name. My first day at Rosyth primary school was memorable for all the wrong reasons: I somehow managed to climb onto the roof and had to be rescued by the janitor. I was belted by the headmaster, the first in a long line of punishments handed down by the authorities.

My first fight also took place at Rosyth primary. It was the classic bully-tries-to-steal-your-dinner-money confrontation. This lad, who was one of the biggest in our class, had already taken my brother's money off him the day before. He no doubt thought that I, being small for my age, would be another easy target. He got the shock of his life. I really battered him. His face was bloodied and I dragged him around the playground as if he was a trophy. It was a huge confidence boost; I had been tested and not been found wanting.

The older I got the more rebellious I became. I was hauled in front of the children's panel on a regular basis. My many offences included shoplifting, vandalism and assault. Another favourite was spray-painting graffiti, a hobby that obsessed me in those days. There are many examples of my handiwork around Inverkeithing and Rosyth, especially my trademark slogan 'Andy. Hibs. Rock and Roll.' It is still visible on gable ends, bridges and public buildings all over town, and it is clearly something I am remembered for if the amount of people who mention it to me is anything to go by. It is therefore not surprising that dad and I were the panel's best customers in those days and I have lost count of the number of times he pleaded with it to keep me out of a children's home. His efforts weren't in vain because the members of the panel, no doubt impressed by a father's commitment to his son, spared me an enforced separation from my family.

Dad tried everything he knew to get me to mend my ways. And don't get the impression he was a soft touch. He wasn't. His father had been strict and dad was too but where I was concerned nothing seemed to work: he grounded me; he told me that I would never get a job; he predicted that I would spend my adult life in jail. Then things really came to a head when I got arrested for the first time at the football. It was 9 February 1980 and Hibs were playing Morton at Easter Road.

After the game I got involved in a fight with away supporters and was picked up by the police and taken to Gayfield Square station. Because I was only fifteen dad had to come and get me. To say he was raging would be a gross understatement. In fact he hit me a skelp before we even got out of the cop shop. His anger had not subsided by the time we got home, where he resorted to a cruel and unusual punishment. He ripped the Hibs posters and pictures off my bedroom wall and put them in the dustbin, knowing it was the worst punishment he could inflict. The next day, when he had gone to work, I retrieved my precious items and carefully concealed them. Just until things cooled down.

Being arrested and contending with dad's anger should have me stop to think. It didn't. If anything I got worse.

I now realise it must have been heartbreaking for dad. It wasn't as if I was no-hoper. In fact I was the brightest of his four children and he must have had a reasonable expectation that I would make something of my life. And of course he was knocking his pan in to put food on the table and a roof over our heads. There were also lawyer's bills to pay from the divorce proceedings and for the custody battles that followed as he did not qualify for Legal Aid. The last thing he needed was a juvenile delinquent to deal with.

At the time I didn't appreciate just how stressful it was for dad but now, with three sons of my own, I do. He had also contested my mother's attempts to get custody of me and my three siblings. Although my sisters went on access visits arranged through the court to my mother's house my brother and I had opted to stay with dad. This undoubtedly put more pressure on him to ensure that I stayed on the straight and narrow. If he couldn't control me and my brother there was always the possibility we would be taken away from him.

As I entered my teenage years my tendency to cause mayhem intensified. I actually made a good start when I moved up to Inverkeithing high school. In my first two years in the big school I was invariably at the top of the class. But when third year came along, and I had to do some real studying, I just didn't make the effort and my academic performance deteriorated sharply. In the playground, by contrast, I was making a real impact. Once again one of the bigger lads picked on me and I gave him a sound beating. The fact that I was small in stature, but had not been afraid to take on an apparently superior opponent, gave me even more street cred. I don't remember having many more playground fights after that. In fact I found that my hard-man reputation had earned me a lot of respect. On the school bus I took the decision to ban my fellow pupils from smoking (a disgusting habit) and they complied, something that the headmaster had failed to achieve despite his best efforts.

I was never one for resting on my laurels and, more importantly, I now had a reputation to maintain. More, and more serious, violence was just around the corner. I was a member of a little gang made up of boys from Rosyth and Inverkeithing; it included Kano, Trotter, Gordon D, Beanz, Davy C and Eddie L. Our first confrontation came when I beat up a boy from one of Inverkeithing's most notorious families. His brothers, who had all left school, vowed revenge and with some of their pals in tow they came to the high school one lunch time. They were bigger, stronger and older than us but we quickly got the upper hand and chased them out of the school gates and right down the high street.

By the age of sixteen, no doubt naively, I considered myself quite the hard man. I also wanted to look the part and so I did what every self-respecting street fighter of the time was doing: I became a skin-head. I just loved the look. The Crombie coats, the Harrington jackets, the Ben Sherman shirts, the fourteen-hole Doc Marten boots. I customised my boots by having one lace green and the other white; it was my little tribute to Hibs. I was so proud of my new identity that I started to tell the world about it through my spray-painting, a habit that would cause me not a little grief. When I was sixteen I painted 'You are now entering skinhead territory' on the gable wall of a house and got sixty days in jail for my pains. (The slogan is still visible nearly thirty years later, despite the fact that it has been painted over.)

But the best thing about being a skin was the reaction from other people: other boys would shite themselves when they saw you and of course that was the whole point of the gear; it made you look aggressive, like a warrior. Girls, on the other hand, let's be honest – it turned them on. I am sure they all fantasised about getting fucked by a skinhead and I did my level best to turn that fantasy into reality. Just read that novel about skinheads where the middle-aged barmaid can't wait to drop her knickers for the main character. It's as good a way as any to meet girls.

I soon discovered there were were more formidable gangs to tackle than a few cunts who turned up at Inverkeithing high school. There was a particularly big one in the local area; one that I realised would take a lot of stopping. It was called the Royal Navy. Rosyth and Inverkeithing were dominated by the naval dockyard, which meant that there were always sailors in town; mainly British, but also American, Canadian, Dutch, French, you name it. Hundreds, often thousands, of the bastards. In any other context I would have nothing against them; after all they were putting their necks on the line to defend this country and our way of life.

The problem was that no group of young men was ever going to accept their town being taken over by another group of young men from outside the area. Especially when the local group is for the most part Scottish and the interlopers are for the most part English. That was throwing fuel on the fire. In addition they had well-paid jobs and most of us were on the dole. This was the late Seventies, early Eighties. Maggie Thatcher was in power and it was hard, if not impossible, for teenagers to get work. The sailors, with money to spend, did what young men everywhere do: they drank, fought, made a nuisance of themselves and took over the pubs, clubs and restaurants. And, worst of all, they shagged our birds. Locals faced an uphill battle to pull because women were drawn like moths to a flame to men in sailor suits, especially ones with exotic accents.

I was angry at the presence of the senior service in our little town. We all were. Something would go off almost every weekend. One night, in the Palace (a cinema that had been transformed into a nightclub) we went toe to toe with a group of young sailors and I vividly remember local boys jumping off what would have been the upper circle to enter the fray. But the most vicious fights always seemed to take place in the Crossroads area of Rosyth, which, with its late-night Chinese takeaway, was a magnet for punters spilling out of the local pubs at closing time. There was also a taxi rank, which had big queues at weekends, and it was more often than not a flashpoint as locals and sailors jostled drunkenly for a cab home.

I remember one Saturday night at Crossroads there was a melee with the sailors and one of them, a really mouthy cunt, jumped into a taxi, hoping to escape. From the safety of the taxi he gave us the finger and a mouthful of abuse. Just at that moment, I saw one of my mates coming out of a public toilet and heading for a pedestrian crossing. I shouted at him to press the button for the lights, which he did. The lights turned to red, the taxi had to stop and we raced towards it before the lights could change again. We dragged the sailor out and gave him a kicking for his troubles. The cops heard about the incident and, a few days later, arrested us. But because they could not identify the sailors all we were charged with was damaging one of the lights on the cab.

Another night we were scrapping outside the Chinese when the owner, clearly exasperated by the constant mayhem outside his premises, stormed out and struck up a pose like David Carradine in the television series *Kung Fu*, which was very popular at the time. He obviously fancied himself as a martial-arts expert and I have to admit he did look the part. But how tough would he be if he was put under pressure? I decided to find out. I walked up, confronted him, and when he did nothing, I stuck the head on him. He groaned and then dropped like a stone to the pavement. After that I never had the same sense of awe when I watched *Kung Fu*.

I also came up with a way of discouraging the sailors from getting off with local women. I arranged for girls I knew to chat them up in the pub, let the sailors buy them drinks and generally give them the come on. At closing time they would call in at the Chinese restaurant and then walk down to Rosyth's public park. With a bellyful of beer and a friendly young girl in tow I have no doubt the sailor boys had more than chop suey on their minds. The plan was that the girl would manoeuvre her companion along a path that ran between the two sections of the park, known locally as the Middle Walk. There were no cars allowed on the Middle Walk so once they were down there they were very much on their own.

Meanwhile a group of us would hide behind the public toilets and when the happy couple walked past we would jump out and start an argument with the sailor. Our girl would keep quiet, so that her 'boyfriend' didn't know she was in on it. Some of the sailors were petrified and immediately offered us their money and their watches, before we even had a chance to ask for them. Others fought like tigers and it often turned very nasty indeed. On one occasion a sailor was joined by his shipmates and during the course of a huge rammy one of them got part of his ear bitten off. Some of our boys were caught and charged and ended up being tried in the High Court.

We had a pretty decent gang in those days. There was a hard core of about twelve game boys, aged between fifteen and sixteen. We began to spread our wings. Dunfermline, the biggest town in Fife, was a favourite haunt. It also had the best shopping centre so we often hung around there, drinking, stealing and fighting. Anything to make a nuisance of ourselves. A keen rivalry soon developed with Dunfermline's many youth gangs, especially the boys from Abbeyview, perhaps Fife's toughest housing scheme. Their gang was known as the AV Toi (short for 'Abbeyview town of independence'). Our clashes with the AV Toi became more and more vicious and things came to a head when two Rosyth lads got jumped by the Toi in Dunfermline. They took a lot of punishment. It was a cowardly act and one that could not go unpunished.

A few nights later about thirty of us went to Abbeyview. We marched across the golf course that separates Rosyth and Abbeyview and found the Toi hanging around the local chippy. We steamed in and gave them a good seeing to. In a blind panic some of their boys ran into a house. We smashed the windows, dragged them out and leathered them. The next night, emboldened by our triumphant incursion into enemy territory, we went back to Abbeyview. Only this time the bizzies were waiting. As soon as the fighting started they lifted me and ten of my mates. I was remanded in Edinburgh's Saughton prison. At the tender age of sixteen I was in an adult nick, one with real criminals. I had always fancied myself as a hard man but now I was mixing with guys who were the real deal, not just little boys out for a punch up. I was a very small fish in a very big pond. Despite this I made some good contacts in Saughton, most notably with the Livingston punks, who were led by a boy called Figs, now sadly deceased. In the years to come the CCS would form strategic alliances with the Livi punks in ventures such as drug dealing, door security and extortion.

At my trial in Dunfermline Sheriff Court I pleaded guilty and was sentenced to three months. My sentence was to be served in a 'DC' – Glenochil detention centre to be precise, a prison for juveniles in central Scotland halfway between Edinburgh and Glasgow. Some of the other gang members also got jail time for the same offences and we were assigned to cells on the second landing, while the Abbeyview boys were one floor above on landing three. Inevitably, there was friction after what had happened on the outside but there were a number of older boys from Abbeyview doing time and they warned both groups to behave. We did as we were told. After all we were only sixteen and at the bottom of the food chain in prison terms. We were under no illusions about what would happen to us if we stepped out of line. Funnily enough, despite the early problems, I became firm friends with the Abbeyview boys and those friendships have endured to this day.

Unlike today – where young offenders seem to enjoy every luxury going from Play Stations to colour tellies – the regime in Glenochil was damn near paramilitary. 'DC' was designed to give young thugs like me a 'short, sharp shock', as it was known at the time. The authorities thought that strict discipline and a demanding routine would jolt us out of our deviant behaviour. In many ways it was like being in a barracks. We had to shave at the same time every morning, whether we needed to or not; our shoes had to be 'bulled' (so highly polished that you could see your face in them); we were expected to iron our clothes carefully; and our beds had to be made to a standard known as a bed block. Then on a Sunday we donned on our BBs or Best Blues, which consisted of a shirt, black trousers and a donkey jacket. The donkey jacket came in useful for the screws. They used it to test for dust under our beds and if there was even one speck on the jacket you were in trouble.

Everything was timed to the second, never mind to the minute. If you needed a crap, even that bodily function was allocated a certain amount of time. We also had to march every day, just like new recruits on a parade ground. I had no problem in adjusting. I have always been a very neat and tidy person and a spell in the Boy's Brigade had given me a degree of familiarity with marching.

Some boys were not so fortunate. Away from home for the first time they struggled with such a regimented way of life. And there was no leeway for those who didn't meet the standards required. If you didn't measure up you could expect a beating from the screws. I have been in places that I would classify as cons' jails, but Glenochil was very much a screw's nick. They ran it with the proverbial rod of iron, and we had to address them at all times as 'sir'. If they suspected you of even a minor infraction – for example, of speaking to another prisoner – they would lash out with fists, boots or whatever they had to hand. For more serious 'offences', like not being able to march properly, they would drag a boys into a cupboard and give them a real going over.

And by Christ we had to work hard. After rising at seven we ate breakfast at half-past and started work at eight. My job was stripping down old transistor radios, a pointless and boring exercise that used to drive me to distraction. Try doing that for eight hours a day. For the first two weeks inside we couldn't even watch television. We were banged up in our cells at night with only the Bible to read. Then we graduated to what was known as blue grade, which meant we were allowed to go to the television room, where we watched a black-and-white set for a couple of hours before returning to our cells for lights out at nine. A few weeks later we were 'promoted' to red or yellow grade, which brought with it an entitlement for the colour-television room.

But if there was one thing that screws and cons agreed on it was on how to treat sex offenders, or 'beasts' as we preferred to call them. One day at work I saw a beast going to the toilet and so I asked the screw permission to go for a slash, which was granted. I went into the cubicle with the beast, battered him senseless and went back to my place. The screws found the beast lying injured on the toilet floor but although they knew I had done it they took no action. They hated those animals as much as I did.

The other main irritation in Glenochil was the Glaswegian. In numerical terms the Weegie was dominant and he never let the boys from the east of Scotland forget it. If you wanted any kind of life you had to stand up for yourself and that meant going toe to toe with the bastards. You could never show weakness and I reckon I did more fighting in DC than I ever did on the outside. It could start at any time for almost any reason. We rarely needed an excuse.

How would I sum up Glenochil? The Ritz it was not. All in all DC was a fucking horrible experience. No home comforts, no home cooking, no women and worst of all no Hibs. At the end of my three months I vowed that I would never be coming back. Life was just too short to spend in a place like that. My mind was made up.

But look how wrong you can be.

2
THE SKINHEAD YEARS

I was determined to stay out of trouble after being released from DC. And I did, for all of twelve hours! As usual I just couldn't help myself: I was hyperactive as a teenager and I probably still am. I am not one for sitting at home and watching the telly; I always have to be out and about. So that night, after saying goodbye to Glenochil in the morning, I found myself at the Crossroads in Rosyth battling with the sailors. Inevitably, I was lifted and half an hour later found myself standing at the charge bar in Dunfermline police station, being told to remove my shoes and belt and to empty my pockets. Quite clearly, my mindset was still in detention-centre mode, as the following exchange shows:

'Name?' barked the desk sergeant.

'Blance, sir.' I replied.

'Where have you been? What's with the "sir" pish?'

'I'm just out of Glenochil this morning.'

'A lot of fucking good that did you,' he rather wearily concluded.

After that I was public enemy number one in the eyes of the local Old Bill. I got arrested constantly, sometimes for things I had done, other times it was just the cops looking to tidy up their books. It was no life. I soon came to the conclusion that a change of scenery was called for and at the age of seventeen I left Fife for Edinburgh, where of course most of my Hibs-supporting pals lived. At first I stayed with a friend and his wife but after a few weeks I moved to bed-and-breakfast accommodation in Leith. This was not twenty-first century Leith with its expensive apartments, trendy restaurants and designer shops. It was early-Eighties Leith, the Leith of Irvine Welsh's *Trainspotting*, the Leith of junkies, prostitutes, high unemployment and dingy council estates. Although officially part of the city of Edinburgh, Leith, with its docks and proud maritime traditions, still retained a strong sense of identity and was a million miles away from Edinburgh's affluent suburbs and exclusive shops. More importantly, for me at least, Leith is the spiritual home of Hibs.

One of the first people I met was James Girvan, who was staying in the same bed and breakfast. He was also a skinhead and a Hibby and we hit it off from the word go. In fact he is still one of my best pals more than quarter of a century later. Girvan is one of the most courageous boys I have ever had the privilege of knowing. Other mobs quickly got to know him, simply because he was such a game cunt. They even gave him a nickname: Skinhead Joe. Later, when the CCS got going and we had become casuals, we called him Mad-Dog-on-a-Leash and later Stormin' Norman. I have so many great memories of Girvan. He always seemed to be on a suicide mission, like the time he steamed into a hundred Dunfermline when there were only four of us. Over the years we have been in so many tight spots. There is no one I would rather be in the trenches with. Respect, big man.

Like many of my pals I didn't have a permanent job in those days. I worked in a gents outfitters before moving to Edinburgh but I stole so much of the stock that I realised I would have to leave before I got caught. Then I went on a YTS scheme and got a position as a trainee in the city council's wages department. With my aptitude for arithmetic I would have made a good wages clerk but that went out of the window when I was convicted after the fight in Abbeyview. If that sheriff had been slightly more lenient I might have made a go of it.

After that my only official source of income was the dole, which doesn't go very far. So I supplemented my money from the social by making false claims for housing benefit (or whatever it was called in those days). Our landlords were in on the scam, in fact they encouraged us. We split the proceeds with them, which gave me a few extra quid in my pocket for the weekend. And then, of course, there was shoplifting, which was then simply a way of earning pin money but would later become an altogether more serious enterprise.

Before long Girvan and I were part of a skinhead gang that numbered around thirty. As usual I was one of the most dedicated members and I went out of my way to act and look the part. I got my hair cut by a barber in Drummond Street, and, to ensure I was completely bald, supplemented his handiwork by taking a razor to my scalp. I had tattoos in all the right places including one on the inside of my lower lip (it read 'Fuck Hearts') and two on my head. One was on my crown: it was a spider's web; the other, which was just above my forehead, was an illustration of a Saltire with a Lion Rampant in the middle of the flag. Our gang was predominantly male but we also had a few female members. They wore the same gear as the boys but their hair was feathered at the sides and very short on the crown. I am not saying it was free love but I ended up in short, but satisfying, relationships with a few of our female colleagues.

We all loved the lifestyle, the clothes and the thrill we got when we walked up Leith Walk and into the city centre. Our aim was not just to be fashion plates but also to intimidate and no matter how busy it was the crowds on Princes Street parted like the Red Sea to let us through. While some people were apprehensive and kept a respectful distance, many tourists wanted to take our photographs. We were happy to oblige and charged £1 a time for the privilege. And there were also ample opportunities for violence. We clashed with visiting gangs from all over Scotland and I recall that one of our most frequent fixtures was with a skinhead gang from Glasgow. But our most formidable opponents were the Livi punks, many of whom we would later befriend. Quite bizarrely, they used to come through to Edinburgh in an old ambulance, which had been painted black. They would file out of the back door and set about us with knives, hammers and baseball bats.

A favourite haunt was the St James Centre, an ugly, concrete shopping mall that sits between Princes Street and Leith Walk. We spent many a happy afternoon there picking fights, shoplifting and generally causing mayhem. The only problem was the security guards who patrolled the centre and gave us no peace. There was one guy who seemed to have a real downer on skinheads in general and our gang in particular. Any time he spotted us we got our marching orders, which we found really irritating. There was an opportunity to turn the tables on him one evening when the centre was quiet and Mr Nuisance Value was doing a late shift on his own. We grabbed him and started to give him a beating he would remember for a long time. But he broke free, made a dash for his little cabin and locked the door. If he thought that was the end of it he was very much mistaken. We tied a rope round the cabin and started to pull it off its foundations. At the same time we threatened to torch it. Nuisance Value was terrified and screamed for help. By this time we had had our fun and withdrew. After that he never got in our way again – in fact he couldn't even make eye contact with us – and we had the run of the centre.

The main source of our fun was battling at the football and there was one incredible week in the summer of 1984 that began with an arrest in the Highlands, continued with an attack on cops inside Easter Road, went on to a fight with English hooligans and ended with me being savagely beaten in a cell. It all started on Tuesday, 31 July 1984, when Hibs faced Elgin City in a pre-season friendly. With Girvan and a couple of others we drove north in a Ford Escort and reached Elgin without any major dramas. Then, when we parked the car, we noticed that the petrol pipe was leaking and that we were almost of out of fuel. Using our initiative we broke into the yard at the back of the post office and siphoned petrol from a postie's van. Unfortunately some fucking busybody spotted what we were up to and called the cops. Girvan and I got away on foot but the others were caught, charged and released on bail. When we found out they had got out we handed ourselves in and we were also charged and released on bail.

The next day Hibs were to play Forfar so we drove down from Elgin for the game. When we got to Forfar we again needed petrol, so we stopped in front of a parked car. As we were siphoning the petrol we heard the unmistakeable sound of a police car slowly and methodically patrolling the area and promptly jumped back into our car, pretending to be asleep. The cops obviously didn't believe we were sleeping and they banged on the windows and doors until we couldn't ignore them any longer. They asked what we were doing there, searched our car and radioed back to HQ to check for outstanding arrest warrants. They found nothing and started to walk back to their patrol car. At that point, out of the corner of his eye, one of the bizzies saw a trail of petrol trickling down the street. All five of us were arrested, charged with theft and locked up for the night in Forfar police station before appearing in court the next morning. We entered a plea of not guilty and once again were released on bail.

On the Friday night we were back in Edinburgh as Hibs prepared to host Manchester City. We positioned ourselves under one of the floodlighting pylons at the point where the open terracing and the cowshed, which had been designated for the City fans, met. There was a line of police strategically positioned between us and the away fans and despite our best efforts we just couldn't get at them. So we turned to the nearest available target: the Edinburgh polis. There were about thirty in our group and it was a fair old battle. They drew their truncheons and struck out at any of our boys within range; we responded with a volley of stones. Then we moved in closer and got into close combat with the cunts.

I landed many hard punches and kicks on the cops and I found it a much bigger thrill than taking on my fellow hooligans from other clubs. Not only were they authority figures but it was also a way of getting my own back for the way they had treated me over the years, both in Fife and in the city. Skinheads were a target and any time I was stopped in the street the cops were always disrespectful, shouting and swearing and trying to intimidate us. We did our best that night but there were just too many of them and I was nicked and taken to the station. I was charged with carrying an offensive weapon (my belt!), resisting arrest and breach of the peace.

However, I didn't get charged with police assault, a much more serious offence. I believe this was because of the beating they gave me in the cells. It wasn't the first time I had been on the receiving end of police brutality. It had happened to me several times in Fife. Many respectable citizens will just not accept that the police assault prisoners in their custody. Well, they did at that time. With the advent of closed-circuit television, the recording of interviews and new rights for prisoners it is now much more difficult for them to get away with it but they had carte blanche in the early 1980s. So after I was processed and had my belt and shoes removed I was put into a cell on my own. A few minutes later three cops came in. Two of them held me while the other one punched and kicked me, mainly about the body so that the bruises wouldn't show up so clearly. The same thing happened to one of my mates, which led to his father lodging an official complaint. I am convinced that the leniency we were shown was directly related to what happened in the cells that night. I got another result when I went to court: they assumed I was a first offender (it was the days before police computers) and I got off with a fine.

The most notable events of that amazing week were still to come. Despite being arrested three times inside four days, and being duffed up in a police cell, I was well up for Sunday's friendly at Easter Road, which was against our Geordie friends, Newcastle United. After the game we tackled their mob in London Road. Although I was still a skinhead Hibs had a small gang of casuals and we joined forces to take on the common enemy. During the fight, my pal, Tripny, got arrested and having had my fill of cops that week I stuck one on the arresting officer, allowing Tripny to get away. The cop staggered back and then made an attempt to radio for assistance. I immediately ripped the radio off his jacket and Tripny and I bolted.

We didn't get far. By this time the area was flooded with bizzies. Tripny and I were arrested and taken to Gayfield Square police station where I was charged with assaulting a police officer, helping a prisoner to escape, damaging police property and breach of the peace. I was kept in the cells until the Tuesday when I pleaded guilty to all charges. Then I got a stroke of luck. For some reason, perhaps because of an administrative glitch, there was no record of my previous convictions and I walked out of the court with a fine.

As I left court that day the thought crossed my mind that my private war with the boys in blue might have finally run its course. It hadn't, not by a long chalk.

It was 27 October 1984. We were playing Hearts away and I was part of a mob of about thirty casuals and skinheads drinking in a pub called Luckies, which is close to Tynecastle. There is always a great expectation that something special will go off before or after the Edinburgh derby and I had a feeling in the pit of my stomach that this was going to be a day that we would remember for a long time to come. I was right.

The first spat was with the bar staff in Luckies. An argument flared with the publican and a glass was thrown at a light on the wall by one of our lads. The whole electrical system fused and we then proceeded to trash the place. I have rarely seen a place being destroyed so efficiently: we smashed glasses, broke tables, threw chairs at the big mirrors, stole bottles of spirits from behind the bar and even raided the cellar. With that we left the pub and made our way to Tynecastle. Then, as we were crossing the road, a car full of Hearts boys tried to run a few of us over. They were pissing themselves. Smart cunts. Our response was decisive. When the car got stuck in the heavy match-day traffic we turned it on its side, trapping the four occupants. Seconds later a Hearts-supporters bus passed and its occupants just couldn't resist giving us the finger and mouthfuls of abuse. We went for the double and tried our best to push the bus over on its side. Although we had no chance of achieving our objective the Scum inside didn't know that and were shiting themselves.

By now there was total fucking mayhem all around us. We heard the inevitable sirens and knew the Old Bill were on their way. But they had a problem. The street was so clogged with cars and pedestrians that only a couple of motorcycle cops could get through. We legged it and reasoned that if we stayed on the pavement the bike cops would not be able to get to us. But one daft polisman was determined to make a name for himself; he mounted the pavement and chased us, despite the fact there were women with prams, children and innocent bystanders in his path. Someone could have been seriously injured or even killed and my first thought was that I had to take him out. As he drew alongside me I saw my chance and dragged the bastard right off his bike. I remember him screaming in agony as he twisted in mid-air and fell heavily to the ground. With Evel Knievel out of action it seemed like I was going to get away but thirty or forty yards ahead the Old Bill had set up a roadblock. They were waiting for me; one of the motorbike boys must have radioed ahead.

My next stop was the cells. I knew what was coming next. They were no doubt thinking that I could have done serious damage to their pal on the bike and that could not go unpunished. This time four of them appeared in my cell and proceeded to knock fuck out of me.

They hit me with truncheons, with their fists and with their feet. As the blows rained down I remember one of them shouting, 'This is for our fucking mate who is lying in the hospital.' Fair enough. I would have done the same for one of my mates.

I was held in the cells for the weekend and hauled before the sheriff court on the Monday morning. I pled not guilty to all charges and was later found not guilty for the bus, not proven for the car but guilty for the motorbike. In terms of my guilty plea, I really had no option because an off-duty cop said he had seen me pull his colleague off the bike. I certainly hadn't spotted any other bizzies in the vicinity.

But who am I to argue with the Old Bill?

3
A LEGEND IS BORN

By the end of 1984 I realised that things had to change. Being a tattoo-covered skinhead was making me way too conspicuous. It was now almost as hot for me in Edinburgh as it had been in Fife. I was the face the police looked for, the first to be arrested. And once they had lifted me there were the beatings down at the nick, which seemed to be getting more and more savage. There is only so much a body can stand. I didn't know what the solution was, but I knew had to find one. And fast. I didn't want to stop going to the football; I certainly didn't want to stop fighting. Nor was I prepared to become a fuddy-duddy scarfer. The clothes were an important part of who I was; my badge of identity. Luckily for me the answer was out there. It became known as the Capital City Service.

    I am not quite sure about the precise origins of the CCS. My own involvement in organised football violence can be traced back to a Hibs-supporters bus that was hired from an Edinburgh company, Liberton Travel. The hire, the collection of dues and all the organisational matters were taken care of by an older Hibs fan called Dougie. By the age of fifteen I had stopped going on the train to away matches and instead took the Liberton bus. Many of my fellow passengers were around the same age and going regularly to games we got to know each other pretty well. We got into quite a few scrapes, as boys of that age do. It was nothing to write home about and consisted mainly of stealing from motorway service stations and minor skirmishes with home fans of the same age. It was kid's stuff, hardly surprising given our tender years. Even our name was on the childish side: we came up with Uncle Dougie's Soccer Hooligans, in honour of Dougie Sneddon, who ran the bus but knew nothing about our fighting and stealing. A moniker like that was hardly going to strike fear into other mobs.

We had some great laughs on the bus. I remember Dougie used to have a whip-round for the driver, using his old Hibs tammy to collect the money. He counted up the cash and then would announce the total in a disappointed tone of voice:

'The driver got £12.31. Thanks very much you shower of miserable bastards.'

After that we knew what was coming when he got up to make his little announcement, so we got in before him: 'Thanks very much you shower of miserable bastards' we would chant when he had counted the money and declared the total. As for kids they got to travel free, but only if they lay down on the luggage racks and stayed there.

As we matured the violence got more serious. I remember one dust-up at Broomfield with Airdrie's renowned Section B mob, who were mainly skinheads. Broomfield (now demolished) was a dump, much like the town of Airdrie itself, but the Section B boys certainly did their best to put it on the map. This day they attacked our bus, shattering the windows with bricks and stones. But instead of cowering beneath our seats, which was what they expected, we got out of the bus and faced them head on. It was at least a score draw, maybe even an away win. Whatever the result we had stood up to one of the best mobs in the country and not been found wanting. Girvan, Bongo and I had been right in the thick of the fighting at Airdrie and we must have shown up well because just a few weeks later we got a very intriguing invitation.

It was an invitation that changed our lives forever.

Hibs were playing in Glasgow and, having given up the bus, Girvan and I decided to go through by train. We got on at Haymarket and ended up in the same carriage as thirty or so smartly dressed young men. They weren't skinheads, they certainly weren't scarfers.

So what the fuck were they?

A LEGEND IS BORN

We soon found out. They were the first Hibs casuals. One of their leading lights was a guy from Leith by the name of Robb and two of the other main boys were known to one and all as Skeets and Ashy. I later learnt that Robb had been told about the Hibs skinheads who were getting it on with other firms and had immediately realised we would be handy boys to have around. Now, when we got on that train, he didn't hesitate. After beckoning us over he asked us to join the firm. We didn't have to be asked twice. For me this was manna from heaven. I was now part of a serious mob, one that was willing and able to take on all comers, even Aberdeen, at that time the undisputed top dogs in Scotland.

I was impressed by Robb, who seemed to know all there was to know about casuals: where to find other firms, how they fought, what they wore, who their top boys were. He was what you might call a guru for casuals. Like me he is not the tallest but he is a game guy, always to the fore when it kicked off. If anyone deserves to be called the founder of the CCS, it is Robb. Perhaps surprisingly his involvement didn't last for that long and I don't think he was still active in the 1990s. Clearly, his life had moved on.

The clothes worn by Robb and his pals were also a huge attraction and not just because they made us less conspicuous than the skinhead outfits. They were only interested in quality gear, gear that was stylish, expensive and sophisticated, clothes that you would be seen dead in. Within a few weeks there were visible changes in the way I looked. I ditched the Doc Martens, the Ben Sherman shirts and the stapress trousers and replaced them with Trim Trab trainers, Pringle sweaters and bleached jeans. That lot would cost you a fortune. Not that I paid for it. I stole my clothes from Edinburgh's most exclusive shops. My hair grew back, covering the tattoos on my crown. The skinhead days were over.

Before long many of the boys from Uncle Dougie's had joined us in the new mob. We were well on the way to becoming a bona fide casuals mob. The only problem was our name. We later called ourselves the Family and our favourite ditty was 'The Hibees Family', which we sang to the tune of the theme song from the American television series, *The Addams Family*. English mobs had adopted names that made them sound serious, even professional, like Inter-City Firm or 6.57 Crew. We needed something in that vein. I don't know who came up with Capital City Service but I liked it immediately. We all did.

A legend was born.

*

Friendship. That to me was the best thing about the Capital City Service. There was of course much else that was memorable. Going to other towns and cities and marching proudly from the city centre to the opposition's stadium was a thrill. Then there were the fights, and the incredible adrenaline rush they gave you; I wouldn't have missed that for the world. Following Hibs, my team, all over Scotland England and the Continent was something I loved, and still do, win or lose.

But most of all I treasure the friends I made in the CCS and I am gratified that so many of us are still close more than a quarter-of-a-century later. They made it all worthwhile. Let me introduce a few of the guys I fought alongside.

James Girvan

What more can I say about 'Stormin Norman' Girvan? We have been in so many tight spots together and with his killer instinct he is invaluable when the chips are down. He is the first guy I phone when I am in trouble. Hard to control at the best of times, Norman can be even more unpredictable when he has sunk a few beers. In fact, excluding myself, there are very few people who can keep him on an even keel after a session in the pub. He was always inclined to steam into a hundred-strong mob when there was just a handful of us.

'Bongo'

I have known Bongo since the age of twelve, when I started to go to Hibs games on my own and we have been close friends ever since. We first met on the Liberton Travel bus, which used to pick me up in Inverkeithing en route to away games. He did run with the CCS but when he was jailed after a fight in Dundee he gave it up. Bongo's real passion has always been Hibs (he was born, and still lives, just a stone's throw from Easter Road) and like me he goes to every game, home and away, and that includes pre-season tours to Europe. You will not find a more committed Hibs supporter anywhere. Bongo is just a genuinely nice guy, someone who would help anyone out, a loyal friend and as honest as the day is long. The only problem is his driving. It's fucking terrible.

'Tattie'

Another friend from my skinhead days in Leith. Girvan and I met Tattie – who hails from Niddrie, one of Edinburgh's hardest schemes – in 1984. He was four years younger than us and he used to follow us around. He was our shadow. But the first time we saw him fight we immediately realised he was a bit special. The boy didn't know the meaning of the word fear. He was ferocious, in my eyes a real psycho. Tattie made a big reputation for himself in our Baby Crew before graduating to the main mob. He is a very useful boy to have around and we all remember the night he stabbed fourteen students with a screwdriver on the Meadows. Why? Because he doesn't fucking like students.

Derek Dykes

Like me Dykes has also written a book on the CCS, *These Colours Don't Run: Inside the Hibs Capital City Service*. He joined the mob a couple of years after Girvan and has always been one of the most prominent members. His brother also ran with us and I can honestly say that they can both handle themselves. His book claims that he has given up fighting at the football but as they say in Scotland, 'I hae ma doubts'.

Sean and Brad Welsh

Brad Welsh was a leading light in the Baby Crew and later in the main mob. He is the better known of the two brothers, simply because he appeared in a *Football Factories* documentary about hooliganism in Scotland, although Sean did feature in a *Panorama* special 'Policing the Casuals', along with me. The company that made the *Factories* series later devoted a whole programme to Brad, his boxing career and his former criminal activities. He was jailed for a fairly lengthy spell for those crimes but after leaving prison he seemed to give up on football hooliganism and go straight. These days he runs a boxing gym.

Mark, Craig and Jack Lynch

These three brothers are all great lads and outstanding fighters. In fact Craig was once a pro boxer and he was very much in the Brad Welsh mould when it came to a scrap, in the sense that he knocked out opponents for fun. Mark was in the original Baby Crew and with guys like him and Brad Welsh on board it is no wonder that they didn't need back up from the main mob. They had an older brother, Don, but he was much too sensible to get involved with the CCS.

Bobby Lipscombe

Bobby is another long-standing member of the CCS. He was with us when we went to Millwall and ended up being sentenced to several years inside on a charge of mobbing and rioting. I went down to London to give evidence on his behalf, a move that backfired spectacularly when the judge demanded to know why the court should believe a thug like me. In hindsight it probably wasn't the smartest move I ever made and it certainly didn't do Bobby much good! A great guy.

Ian Horan

I first met Horan when he was working as a road-sweeper with the council. His cart had CCS written on it! Recognising a kindred spirit we became good friends. He was a happy-go-lucky guy, full of life and laughter, his mission in life to cheer people up. Sadly, he died several years ago. My abiding memory of him is the day he was working down a hole in Dunfermline town centre and spotted a witness who was to give evidence against the CCS. Horan leapt out of that hole in the ground and, still wearing a big pair of wellies, chased the cunt with a hammer. Sadly, he passed away a few years ago. I still miss him.

Terry 'Tel Boy' Reilly

From Royston in Edinburgh, Tel Boy was a born criminal with convictions for armed robbery, extortion, kidnapping and murder. He was also a hell of a fighter and one of the boys who made the Baby Crew so formidable. He died in June 2009.

Taylor

I first met Taylor when we became next-door neighbours in Soutra Court in Gracemount. A fellow passenger in Uncle Dougie's bus he graduated to the CCS at the same time as me and became one of its most prominent members. I always think of him as the Peter Pan of the mob. He is one of those lucky bastards who never seems to age.

Mikey Neri

One of the youngest members of the original CCS, Mikey is a handy guy to have around. He was, and is, a big, brawny lad and when he hits you, believe me, you stay hit. With his shock of blond hair and his size he always sticks out a mile. Mikey is proud of his Irish Catholic heritage, which makes him almost unique in CCS circles.

James 'Fat' McLeod

In the early years he was a good, reliable member. He even featured in an article about the CCS, which appeared in the *Sunday Times* on 11 November 1990, and was one of the boys in the photograph that accompanied the article. But when I went into prison for the attack on the Kronk in 1991 he got it into his head that he should be the leader of the CCS. When that dream turned to dust he was a leading player in the formation of the so-called Scottish National Firm.

4
WHY WE FIGHT

People often say to me, 'You seem like a sensible and intelligent man. So why did you get involved in hooliganism?' I wish I had a pound for every time I have been asked that question. It would pay for my season ticket at Easter Road, not to mention the pie and Bovril at half-time. As with so many aspects of life there is no one simple reason. It is a combination of many things.

If there is one thing that unites 99 per cent of casuals it is our interest in clothes. We are all, to a greater or lesser extent, fashion victims. Like the mods and rockers of the Sixties, the punks in the Seventies and the New Romantics of the Eighties the uniform is crucial. For them it was parkas, bovver boots or Mohican haircuts. For us it is designer-label clothes.

In the early days Pringle jumpers, Trim Tab trainers and bleached jeans were all the rage. Later we got into Benetton, Pop 84, Chevignan, Lacoste and, a particular favourite, Burberry. We got ideas for clothes from everywhere: London, magazines like *The Face*, celebrities. Boris Becker wore Sergio Tacchini tracksuits, so we did too. As the years passed we moved upmarket, latching onto expensive labels like Armani, Paul Smith and Paul and Shark. There were some more outlandish outfits: I remember a few of us marching through Glasgow wearing tweed jackets and deerstalker hats.

In later years it became easy to spot a casual just because of the brands he had on. Sometimes those brands confused the Old Bill, particularly those that had yet to reach the mass market. In the mid 1980s one or our guys, Tottenham John, (who lived in Edinburgh but was originally a Spurs boy) got into a fight with Celtic in Glasgow. He was arrested and, as the handcuffs were put on, Tottenham John heard the cop say, 'We've got the top boy. He's got Boss written on his sweatshirt.' The daft bastard had never heard of Hugo Boss.

The fashion industry has a lot to thank casuals for, despite the fact that we nicked their products on a regular basis. When we started wearing a new label people would come up and ask: 'What the fuck is that you've got on?' Three months later everyone was buying it.

It is hard to pick out a favourite brand, one that we preferred above all others. But if I was pushed I would go for Stone Island. I started wearing it in the early 1990s and by the middle of the decade it had grown enormously. Now it is everywhere. My favourite jacket of all time was a Stone Island. It had a hood and balaclava, with an inner jacket. When the hood and balaclava were in place all you could see was my eyes and mouth. So as well as looking good it was ideal for avoiding being identified during a ruck. I sold that jacket after being charged with serious offences at the Kronk. I knew jail time was almost inevitable so it was the sensible thing to do. All the same it broke my heart.

The only problem with fashion was that some boys put on a Stone Island jumper and thought they were casuals. We never lost sight of the fact that the most important thing was having the ability to fight and the courage to back up your mates. Some people turned up looking like a dummy from Burton's window in the least fashionable clothes you could imagine but we accepted them if they were game.

Enjoying a scrap is something is something that unites *real* casuals. There is nothing like steaming in with your hair on fire. I have never taken drugs but boys who have tell me that it just doesn't compare with the adrenaline rush you get from attacking a really good mob. As for sex it doesn't even come close.

Apart from fashion and fighting what else drew us into the hooligan world? There is an element of male bonding. Just like the army or the mafia! In fact I have often thought that walking as a mob to Celtic Park or Ibrox must be similar to soldiers marching on foreign soil. The sense of togetherness is special. You are part of something, you have a common goal. It lifts the spirits. We looked after each other too. When we heard that other firms had set up funds to pay fines we did the same and I was given the job of collecting the dues. The way it worked was that, so as long as you were up to date with the weekly payments, the fund would pay any fine levied by the courts. It worked really well, that is until Ashy got a £600 fine after a battle in Falkirk. It was a huge sum for the Eighties and it ended up bankrupting the fund!

There was a whole range of social activities. The CCS even had its own football team. It was called Meadow Albion and it competed in the Maybury Sunday League. Although I wasn't in the team (I am crap at football) many of our top boys were, including Girvan, Taylor, Mark Lynch, Bobby Lipscombe and Cashzie. With a line up like that you expect fireworks and that is exactly what we got. One afternoon Meadow Albion were playing a side called Queensferry Hearts, a name that was a red rag to the proverbial bull. With the tackles flying in and insults being exchanged it was only a matter of time before things got out of hand. One of our boys got into an argument with his immediate opponent and fairly skelped him. Touch-paper lit there was a melee involving all twenty-two players and it spread to the adjacent pitch, where another team with Scum sympathies was playing. The end result was that both games were abandoned and Meadow Albion was thrown out of the league.

During another game Bobby Lipscombe was sent off and ended up whacking the referee, who, to his credit, got stuck right back into Bobby. They eventually managed to get Bobby to go off and in the quiet of an empty dressing room his resentment at the way he had been treated grew and grew. He jumped in his van, drove it onto the pitch and tried to run the poor old ref down. And they say professional referees have a hard life!

Friendship is especially important. Despite the image the world has of me I cherish my friends and go out of my way to help them. When CCS boys were jailed I made sure they weren't forgotten. I wrote to them, visited them and collected money from the rest of the mob to buy them trainers, clothes and other little treats. If you know people on the outside are rooting for you it makes jail time so much easier to bear. Even my worst enemy would have to concede that I am a popular and sociable person. I recently checked my mobile and discovered that I had 1,112 contacts listed. While many of them are business acquaintances most of them are friends, people that I genuinely value. It is said that if you have friends, real friends, you can bear any cross. I happen to believe that.

There is something else. Something that is far more important than anything I have mentioned so far. We fought for the love of Hibs. We wanted Hibs to have the best mob in Scotland, to be number one on and off the field. Why go into something if you don't want to be the best? It was a question of pride, of loyalty to your team. I remember when Rangers and Celtic used to come to Edinburgh and take over our city. It was humiliating. Even worse was the way Hibs fans were picked on by the Gorgie Aggro any time we happened to be playing at Tynecastle. Hibs fans were a soft touch, they were victims who more often than not had to either hide their scarves or leave them at home. We changed all that.

A casual from another mob put it best. He said: 'A true lad fights not because he hates what is in front of him but because he loves what is behind him.' My sentiments exactly.

Frank Dougan is a well-known Hibs man. As treasurer of the Hibs Supporters Association he is often asked to give a fan's perspective to the newspapers, radio and television. Frank hates football violence but he acknowledges that before the CCS Hibs scarfers got a hard time.[1] He remembers coming out of Ibrox one time and helping an elderly lady (Frank thinks she was in her eighties) down the stadium steps. She was wearing a green anorak, not a Hibs anorak, just an ordinary Marks and Spencer-type jacket. But because it was green she was getting vile abuse from a few Rangers fans. A CCS boy saw what was happening and punched one of her tormentors in the mouth. When Frank turned round he saw that the bluenose's face had been burst wide open. That put a swift end to the abuse.

---

[1] In fact Frank and his association passed a resolution condemning CCS violence.

My pal Bongo agrees that scarfers have a lot thank us for, although he has noticed a definite change in their attitude over the years:

> At first they [Hibs scarfers] liked the CCS because they were no longer attacked everywhere they went, regardless of which ground. But their principles have changed. They have forgotten what ordinary fans had to go through before the advent of the casuals. I think that most of them have short memories and are ungrateful. Without the CCS they would have got a lot more beatings.

Bongo should know. He is a former member of the CCS and a Hibs fanatic who has probably attended more of the club's games than anyone else over the last twenty-five years. Scarfers, even those who dislike us and the things we do, would have to acknowledge that thanks to the CCS the world is a safer place for Hibs fans.

Will we get any credit? I am not holding my breath.

5
LOVE AND MARRIAGE

The move from being a skinhead to a casual in late 1984 was a defining moment in my life. But there was an even more important event at that time: I met my future wife. We ran into each other for the first time when I went for a night out with a pal, Alma, in her home town of Prestonpans. There was a crowd of us in the pub and as the evening progressed I became more and more engrossed in my conversation with a local girl called Margo. We had very similar personalities: friendly, open, talkative and we got on like the proverbial house on fire right from the off.

It went so well that I was soon on the phone to ask her out. She accepted and we arranged to meet in a pub called Arthur's, which was in one of the lanes off Edinburgh's Royal Mile. It wasn't what you might call a conventional first date. During the course of the evening I helped trash a pub, got into two fights, was chased by the filth, kicked in a shop window and was arrested. Then there was my encore.

Defecating on the floor of a police cell.

It seemed to go tits up from the word go. We were part of a group of casuals, skinheads and their women having a quiet drink. Then a group of skinheads from Glasgow marched in. I wondered what the fuck they were doing there but it turned out my past had once again caught up with me. I had had sex with the girlfriend of one of their boys and they had come all the way through to Edinburgh to teach me a lesson. All that way for just one ride; those boys really should have got out more. Angry they may have been but when they saw how many of us were in the pub they got cold feet and bottled it. Panic over it was back to the drink.

The spirit of harmony did not last for long. We got into an argument with a group of locals and within seconds the pub was in turmoil. As we went at it with these new opponents tables were overturned, windows broken and the gantry smashed up. The bizzies were on the scene quickly and so we bailed out of Arthur's with a load of cops in hot pursuit. I knew I couldn't outrun them so when I went round a corner I saw my chance and dived underneath a van.

It worked. They ran right past. When the coast was clear I went back to the pub to see how Margo was.

On the way, purely by coincidence, I bumped into Girvan and we walked back to Arthur's together. When we arrived I was pleased to see Margo hadn't deserted me: she was sitting there with some of the other girls, chatting away. We decided that was enough excitement for one night and began the long walk home to Leith. Fate must have had it in for us because when we were crossing North Bridge we saw there was a fight in full swing next to the Waterloo statue. As we got closer we recognised two of our skinhead pals, who were taking a bit of a pasting from three assailants. Without a moment's hesitation Girvan and I ran up and got stuck right in, forcing the three cunts to run. First rule of the CCS: you always back up your mates.

We continued on our journey but we obviously hadn't had our fill of excitement. As we passed a grocer's shop Girvan launched a kick at one of the windows, shattering it into a thousand pieces. In my drunken state I decide that I had better do the other one, which I did. Someone saw us, called the bizzies and we were arrested and taken to the nearest station.

Margo had also been picked up by the police, but as a witness. When she was questioned the cops wouldn't let her go to the toilet unless she stuck us in for the window incident, which she had no option but to confirm. Meanwhile, in the cells, Girvan and I had both spewed our guts up. Then when they refused us permission to go to the toilet we dropped our trousers and shat on the floor. That got their attention: without further ado we were charged, thrown out of the cells and able to complete our delayed journey back home to Leith.

All in all it was a hell of a first night and I was understandably surprised when Margo agreed to go out with me for a second time. But she did. As time passed we grew on each other and our relationship got stronger and stronger. Like me she came from a hard-working, law-abiding family so I am sure her parents must have got a shock when they first set eyes on me. But if they did they didn't show it. In fact they were very supportive and always tried their best to keep me on the straight and narrow. It was an impossible task.

My past once again came back to haunt me. Not long after Margo and I became an item I was arrested for stealing copper. A mate and I had sneaked into a builder's yard one night and helped ourselves to a huge load, so big in fact that we sold it for £5,000. I was tried on 8 January 1985, found guilty and remanded in custody pending social-enquiry reports. I was probably looking at a prison sentence but due to a tragedy in the life of my co-accused I got away with a much lighter punishment. While we were on remand my accomplice's baby died. He immediately got bail on compassionate grounds and then at his sentencing hearing he was given community service. With his record, which was much worse than mine, he would have been sent to prison nine times out of ten. Three weeks later I was in the dock for sentencing. My lawyer argued that I should also get community service because my co-accused had a much worse record, conveniently forgetting to mention that it was because of the baby's death. Maybe the sheriff didn't know about my pal's bereavement, or maybe he did but for some legal reason couldn't give me a harsher punishment, but whatever the reason I also got community service, which, when all is said and done, is a piece of cake compared to prison.

Although I walked free from court the case had shocked Margo's parents. They realised how serious our relationship had become and the last thing they wanted was a jailbird for a son-in-law. So they asked me to come and stay with them, thinking it would help me stay out of trouble. I moved in and then something even more momentous happened shortly thereafter. Margo got pregnant. Her mum took the view that we should get married without delay. We refused, telling her that we wouldn't be forced into anything. That didn't go down too well; I was kicked out of the house in Prestonpans and found myself back living in a Leith bed and breakfast.

It didn't keep us apart. We continued to see each other and when our son, Kevin, was born we were allocated a council flat in my home town of Inverkeithing. The flat was in Fraser Avenue, then as now one of the toughest streets in the county of Fife. We eventually did get married, in August 1986, and a few months later, in January 1987, our second son, Jamie, arrived.

Having a wife and a young family should have changed me. It didn't. I was still just as active in the CCS, perhaps more so. Margo, of course, didn't like me getting into trouble. It worried her sick. She never knew when I would be coming home, or even if I would be coming home. On a Saturday evening I was just as likely to end up in a prison cell or on a hospital ward as I was to walk through the front door. Then there were the threats, which during periods of tension with other mobs came on an almost daily basis. They weren't just made against me; my family was also threatened.

There is one incident that typifies those years. In the summer of 1988 I was on trial in the High Court for very serious offences, including mobbing and rioting. I was on bail and when the trial broke up on the Friday I told Margo I was going down to Oldham with the mob for a pre-season friendly. She was livid.

'You can't go down to Oldham. You're in the middle of a High Court trial,' was her understandable reaction.

'I have to. Everyone else is going.'

When I got up the next morning I couldn't find any shoes. Margo had hidden them all. She really didn't want me to go to Oldham. But a little thing like that wasn't going to stop me. I went round to a pal's house and borrowed a pair of trainers. Nor did my trial stop me from getting involved when I got to Lancashire. In fact it turned out to be one of the most violent of our away days, with fights in Manchester and Oldham.

That was probably the beginning of the end for our marriage, although we limped along in much the same vein for another couple of years. Looking back I now realise I caused Margo a lot of worry and a lot of heartache. No wife or mother should have to put up with that. I regret it, just as I regret the hurt I caused my father and other members of my family.

6
WHEN ONE DOOR CLOSES...

I suppose it was inevitable that I would find work as a doorman, or bouncer, or steward, call it what you will. I have stood on doors all over the east of Scotland: in Inverkeithing, Edinburgh, Dunfermline, Livingston. For me it was like being on holiday and getting paid for it. The music, the heady atmosphere, the women dressed to the nines and most of all the sense of anticipation you get from being just a heartbeat away from violence. What could be better?

My first job was in Captain Jack's, Inverkeithing's only nightclub worthy of the name. I will always remember my first night there – Boxing Day 1988 – for one very good reason. It was the day, aged twenty-three, I stopped drinking – for good. I had been on the door for about two hours when head doorman Mike Collins – a great guy who later became a close friend – asked if we would like a drink. I opted for a lager but was told that alcohol was not allowed while I was on the door. I had a juice instead. Although we were offered another refreshment at the end of our shift – alcoholic if we so wished – I didn't see the point of having just one drink. I was more used to having five or six as part of a session. So, once again, I had juice and now I won't drink anything else.

To be honest I have never missed alcohol. I had never been a heavy drinker, for the simple reason that it didn't take much to get me drunk. I wasn't the best at holding my liquor and when I did have one too many the consequences were often dire. I was completely unpre-

WHEN ONE DOOR CLOSES...

dictable on the piss and all too often I woke up in a police cell not knowing how the fuck I had got there.

The result was that I always had a clear head on the doors, which was essential in Captain Jack's. It was a fun place but frequently wild and violent. This was mainly due to clashes between the two groups that made up our clientele. On the one hand you had the locals, who, quite understandably, saw Captain Jack's as their spot, somewhere they could go to drink, relax and pick up women. Then there were the sailors and marines who came to our little town in huge numbers while their ships were being refitted in Rosyth dockyard. They were young guys in a strange town with money to spend. For them it was like being on a stag weekend. They were loud, boisterous and very, very horny. They had two goals while they were in Captain Jack's: to get pissed as quickly as possible and then to pull a local bird. Luckily for them some of the Fife girls didn't need a lot of romancing. When it came to opening their legs for men in uniform they didn't have to be asked twice.

Something always went off when the locals were outnumbered by the sailors. It was territorial, a reaction to being overrun on home soil by outsiders. As most of the navy boys were English there was also a natural Scotland–England rivalry thrown into the mix. The sailors tended to be worse than the Royal Marines, who were more disciplined and less inclined to get legless, although when roused they were formidable fighters.

I was thrown in at the deep end from the off. Halfway through my first night a major barney erupted, involving about forty guys on each side. There were only five of us on the door but somehow we coped until the cops arrived and broke it up. It was a scene that would be repeated night after night. It started with punches and kicks, then glasses and bottles would be thrown, while others entered the fray using tables and chairs as weapons. Forgive the cliché but it really was like a saloon in the Wild West.

It wasn't just English sailors and marines we had to contend with. They came from any country that happened to be in NATO: America, Canada, Belgium, Denmark; a real cosmopolitan bunch. From our point of view the worst of the lot were the sailors from Holland. They were hard cunts who had little or no respect for authority. I remember one night in particular when, as was par for the course, we had ejected a group of Dutch from the club.

That's when the fun started.

About half an hour later five of them came back. I was on duty with one other doorman and when we knocked them back they tried to force the door open. We were outnumbered and struggling to keep them out. So I improvised. I took one of the long metal bolts off the door frame and whacked the nearest Dutchman over the head with it. It was a clean hit, one that would have knocked down any normal man. But he was one of those brick-shithouse guys and although he staggered he managed to stay on his feet. Not only had I failed to put him down but I had also made him even angrier.

I thought we were in for a right kicking, or perhaps worse. These guys were very big and very drunk and they had completely lost the plot. A dangerous combination.

We were in luck. Just as they moved in for the kill one of the other bouncers came down the stairs with a punter he was about to throw out. When he saw what was happening he pressed the panic button, alerting two more doormen. Now there were five of us against five of them. We fought them to a standstill until the police arrived and arrested the Dutch boys.

I was always happy at Captain Jack's. I loved the crack, the company and the opportunities it gave me for fighting. It was old school; you hit first and asked questions later. Subtle it was not. As with so many other things in my life it was brought to a shuddering halt by *that* night at the Kronk.

*

I wasn't out of the doorman game for long. In the spring of 1991, while on the run after the Kronk, I started to frequent the South Side snooker centre, which is in Edinburgh near to the Meadows. I got to know the staff and management well, and, after I had been charged with the Kronk and was out on bail, the club asked me to work on the door.

With a bar and function room downstairs and snooker tables

upstairs the Southside was a favourite haunt of the CCS and boys from Edinburgh's roughest estates. With such a rowdy clientele it soon earned a justified reputation as one of toughest spots in the city. The management probably thought employing me was a poacher-turned-gamekeeper move that would keep the lid on trouble. And it is certainly true that while I was on the door things were for the most part quiet. That said I experienced two of the hairiest moments of my life while working there.

There was torrential rain this day. From my position just inside the front entrance I saw a boy I knew running at top speed towards the club. He was obviously trying to get out of the rain as quickly as possible so I opened the door, expecting him to hang around for a chat when he got inside. The ignorant bastard didn't even stop to thank me.

I got a sixth sense that something was wrong. I noticed that my friend was as white as a ghost and shaking uncontrollably. A split second later I found out why. A man with a face darker than those rain clouds burst in. But it wasn't his anger that caught my attention.

It was the gun in his right hand.

I didn't have time to think. I grabbed the gunman, threw him to the ground, wrestled the gun from his grasp and bundled him out of the door.

'Don't be so fucking stupid. Don't bring a fucking gun in here,' I shouted, throwing the weapon back to him.

It was instinctive. If I had stopped to think I would have left well alone. This guy was a well-known face in Edinburgh's underworld and he was obviously angry about a deal, probably involving drugs, which had gone wrong. I knew he was well capable of using the shooter. Now all that separated me from him was a pane of glass. Luckily for me he came to the conclusion that to shoot someone in a busy club was probably not a good idea. He put the gun in his jacket and walked away.

My pal couldn't thank me enough. He thought I had saved him from a kneecapping or worse. I was relieved but at the same time I realised it might be a different story the next time I ran into the gunman. Those guys hate to lose face. But when I did see him again he had taken a decision to laugh it off, telling everyone what an idiot he had been. My luck was in.

The second major incident at the Southside didn't involve a gun, but it was equally dangerous. One of the CCS, who was then aged sixteen, was in the club when two radges from Niddrie – one of Edinburgh's toughest schemes – came in and proceeded to give him a hard time. They were much older than our boy, probably in their late twenties. There was neither rhyme nor reason for their behaviour. He had done nothing to them. They were just being annoying cunts.

The situation became more and more heated. Then I saw one of them had pulled a knife and was threatening the teenager. So I walked over and said:

'Pick on someone your own age.'

'Well you're our fucking age,' one of them replied.

'Any fucking time you like pal,' I retorted in my most menacing tone.

The radges backed down and returned to their seats, cursing me, my pal and the CCS.

In the meantime the young lad had phoned his two older brothers. They told him to wait for ten minutes then to go over and start an argument with the Niddrie boys. He did and when they lost their cool he pretended to be afraid and ran out of the club. The Niddrie-ites gave chase, knives at the ready. But when they got outside they were met by my pal's brothers. One of the brothers had a sword underneath his jacket and when he pulled it out he compared it to the radges' knives:

'Call that a knife,' he said, scornfully.

It was just like that scene from *Crocodile Dundee* when Dundee pulls out his big fucking bushman knife and sticks it in the mugger's face. You know the one I mean.

The swordsman slashed one of the Niddrie boys, while the other sibling bludgeoned his opposite number with a hammer. The brothers left them in a deep pool of blood and managed to get away before the law arrived. Of course I was a potential witness and was questioned by the filth, who had two possible attempted-murder cases on their hands. They insisted I must have seen it all but I told them I was in the toilet when it happened!

*

WHEN ONE DOOR CLOSES...

My third stint as a doorman started in 1998, when I joined Niteclub Security, a company owned by a man called Alex McAulay. I worked for Alex at several venues and had impressed him with my handling of outfits like the Falkirk Fear (casuals) and assorted gangs from Livingston. As a reward he made me head doorman at the 1,400-capacity Ballroom in Dunfermline, by some distance the biggest nightclub in the county of Fife.

By now the job had changed out of all recognition. The world had moved on and it was no longer acceptable to get wired into punters, unless it was the last resort. The emphasis now was on communication, persuasion and the use of positive body language. Licensing schemes were more common and you had to do it the right way or face losing your right to work. The other factor was Alex McAulay himself. He pioneered the new methods and provided door staff with intensive training in people management. He told us to treat the punters like friends, to have a laugh and a joke with them. That was how to defuse difficult situations. His training was excellent and for much of the time the new techniques worked a treat.

But the leopard does not change its spots. When frustrated or provoked it will strike. And the same was true of the nightclub patron, especially at midnight when he is full of drink. Despite our expertise in the touchy-feely way of doing things there were occasions when we had to revert to type and just bang heads together. It was then that you sorted the men from the boys. Although we had up to twelve doormen (and two women) at the Ballroom I only ever rated five of them. The rest were cowards who didn't have the hearts they were born with. Sometimes it was the biggest guys, the ones who should have been able to handle themselves, who were the worst.

So it was perhaps just as well that I usually had Mr McAulay to back me up. The guy has bottle, pure and simple. In fact I would say he is the hardest, and bravest, man I have ever met. He was certainly the only one at that club who could pull me into the staff room when I lost the plot. And I was the only one who could control him when he was raging, which was a sight to behold. Alex worked hard at his trade. He went to the gym on a regular basis and was expert in boxing, grappling and wrestling. Not only that. He could disable a full-grown man simply by putting two fingers on the back of his neck, a useful skill for a doorman to have.

We found ourselves in many tight spots but we made a great team and things usually worked out all right. I certainly could have done with him at my side the night I faced my greatest challenge as a doorman, but I think I did okay under the circumstances. It was a Sunday, normally one of the quieter nights at the Ballroom. But it was no ordinary Sunday; it was the day of an Old Firm game. All of a sudden about thirty boys started going at it in the street outside the club, one group Celtic, the other Rangers. It was a vicious fight fuelled by all-day drinking and the twisted hatred that goes hand-in-hand with religious bigotry in Scotland. Even worse, two of the combatants were wielding baseball bats. People have been killed in much less volatile situations.

I rounded up three of the other bouncers and we walked towards the fight. But, as we got closer, my colleagues, faced with probably the most violent scene they had ever witnessed, stopped. They were scared shitless. I kept going and when I got into the middle of the ruck I snatched one of the bats. I prodded it at the group to my left, pushing the rioters back then turned round and did the same to the other group. I was lucky. It worked. If it hadn't I would have got the hiding of my life, probably from both sides. The fight ran out of steam and I just managed to keep the two sides apart until, after a few more minutes, the police belatedly arrived.

The next day the cops came round to the Ballroom and asked the manageress to thank me for what I had done. They knew the situation could easily have escalated with people being maimed or even killed. As they explained to the manageress they had been involved in another incident and couldn't get to the Ballroom as quickly as they would have liked. Of course they didn't thank me in person, which is pretty much par for the course.

I gave up the doors in 2006 but not because I didn't enjoy it any more. The fact was that my family circumstances had changed. My third son Jack was born in 1998 and working at the club meant that as he grew up I couldn't see him or have him to stay overnight.

7
ABERDEEN: JUST A GOOD, HONEST MOB

One cowardly incident apart I have always respected Aberdeen as a mob. They were like us in so many ways – local guys who supported their local team and unlike the Neanderthals who follow the Old Firm there was never any hint of religious bigotry. As a general rule an Aberdeen boy, like us, did not need a weapon in his hand to get it on. That was very much my attitude. Unless you were badly outnumbered, or the opposition pulled a knife, you should rely on fists, feet and head.

In Scotland at least the Aberdeen Soccer Casuals (ASC) were trailblazers for the whole casual movement. The story goes that during the home leg of a European Cup tie against Liverpool in October 1980 some Aberdeen fans observed that a number of their Scouse visitors were wearing designer trackies and expensive trainers. These boys must have seemed so cool compared to the scarfers with their fuddy-duddy 'Christmas tree' look. Inspired by their trendy guests the ASC was born.

I first became aware of Aberdeen in 1983. Their fledgling mob had gone into the Motherwell end at Fir Park, started a fight and given the home fans quite a kicking. The media lapped it up, describing it as a new phenomenon and noting that the Aberdeen boys were togged out in expensive designer gear. I was still a skinhead but I was excited by what had happened at Fir Park, just like the Aberdeen boys had been inspired by the Liverpool casuals a few years earlier. I wasn't the only one. Many of my mates felt the same way. It was around that time we evolved into casuals and that the CCS was born.

Given the ASC was Scotland's only real mob in those days it is not surprising that our first large-scale battle (if you exclude an earlier kicking they gave us at Kirkcaldy) was against them. What we didn't realise at the time was that it was very nearly our last. The date was 23 March 1985. The place was Easter Road. We had a burning desire to be casuals, to be respected, to be feared like the ASC. And as we gathered in the Royal Nip, our spiritual home, that Saturday afternoon we were ready to face them. At least we thought we were ready. The reality was that we didn't have a clue about how to go about it. Uncle Dougie's Soccer Hooligans had been a lark; yes we got into a few tumbles with other gangs but that was strictly small time, almost innocent. We were now going from the third division to the premiership. We were also heavily outnumbered. Aberdeen brought around five hundred boys that day, a lot of them hardened hooligans with many scalps to their name. The CCS by contrast could only muster about fifty. It was a recipe for disaster.

Within minutes of leaving the Royal Nip we saw the ASC. After a few minutes warily eyeing each other up we blinked first and, like headless chickens, steamed in. At first they were taken aback and retreated but when they realised how few of us there were they counter-attacked and swarmed all over us. I had no option but to backtrack, like the rest of our boys. Knowing the area like the back of my hand was a big advantage and I got away, embarrassed by the humiliation of having to run on my own patch. I was unscathed but one of my mates wasn't so lucky.

Raymie Morrell was in the thick of the action but he too was forced to turn tail. Before he did, in act of defiance, he picked up a traffic cone and hurled it at Aberdeen. Then, as he tried to get away, he stumbled and fell to the ground. The ASC were on him in a flash, kicking and punching for all they were worth. I didn't see what happened but it seems that dozens of them, driven by the blood lust of the mob, piled in. Raymie was seriously injured. He took many blows to the body and, more worryingly, to the head. He could easily have been killed. It was a disgusting, cowardly act, perhaps not typical of Aberdeen but a liberty nonetheless.

ABERDEEN: JUST A GOOD, HONEST MOB

Inside Easter Road the rumours spread like wildfire. Raymie was in a coma. Raymie had brain damage. Raymie was dead. Understandably, the atmosphere was poisonous and it wasn't helped by the ASC, who were cock-a-hoop at their exploits. They taunted us, pointing out correctly that we had run away. We were raging, as were the vast majority of Hibs fans. So their fans, scarfers included, were pelted with stones and coins throughout the match, while the Aberdeen players got the same treatment. One of the linesmen was unlucky enough to be in the firing line and he was hit on the head with a stone, at which point the referee was forced to stop the game and to take the players off the field until order was restored.[2]

After the game the coppers, fearing a bloodbath, surrounded the ASC. We did our best to get at them, tracking them all the way to Waverley station but all we had to show for our efforts was battering a few stragglers who we trapped on a walkway. It wasn't nearly enough. That night in the pub we were deflated not just by the rout but also by the manner of it. We had been naive and amateurish and had deserved all we got. After a couple of hours of feeling sorry for ourselves our thoughts turned to revenge. There would be a day of reckoning and it would come at the next Hibs–Aberdeen match, where this time we would make home advantage pay. Although that fixture would not take place for months, in October 1985, what happened that day was never far from our minds.

In the meantime Aberdeen did their level best to keep the fires burning. The ASC insisted on bragging about nearly killing Raymie at every ground they visited. The sick cunts even composed a little ditty, which they sang to the tune of '99 Red Balloons' by Nena:

99 big soccer reds
Bouncing on poor Raymie's head

Fucking comedians.

---

[2] The Aberdeen goalkeeper, Jim Leighton, was hit on the neck with an iron bolt while his colleague Alex McLeish was struck by a coin. In its coverage, the *Sunday Mail*, under the banner headline 'Thug Rule Is Back', reported that the match referee had described the violence as the worst he had ever experienced.

In the book written by former ASC member Jay Allan (*Bloody Casuals: Diary of a Football Hooligan*, 1989) the author states, 'Thank God he [Raymie] didn't die. Nobody, at least nobody I know, wants to kill. It's just a game.' Fair enough Jay – but a lot of your mates obviously didn't feel the same way. If they were genuinely concerned about Raymie why did they write a song about what they had done and then belt it out at every ground in Scotland? Not much sign of remorse there.

They say that every cloud has a silver lining and the attack on Raymie Morrell is proof of that. As the game with Aberdeen approached we were inundated. It seemed that every other Hibs fan wanted to join the CCS, even if it was just for one day. They came from all over Edinburgh and beyond. Even the radges from Niddrie pledged their allegiance to the cause. With reinforcements and a clear strategy we knew it would be a different story this time. But little did we know it would be a day that changed football hooliganism in Scotland forever.

It is hard to convey how strongly we felt about righting that wrong. It was an obsession that bordered on fanaticism. One of our mates had been left for dead and his assailants had the brass neck to brag about it to all and sundry. The gap between the two games also stoked the flames. It gave us ample time to brood on our inadequacies. Aberdeen had been right about one thing. We did run away. And that was the hardest thing of all to accept. Something special was called for. Something that would do more than just wipe the slate clean; a disproportionate response. I don't know who it was that came up with the idea of petrol bombing the cunts but I thought it was a stroke of genius. And I didn't hear any dissenting voices. We all loved the idea. Those sheep-shagging bastards had to be taught a lesson they would never forget.

On the day of the game we decided to keep our powder dry until after the match. We were about to try something spectacular and we hoped it would lull Aberdeen and the Old Bill into a false sense of security. There was the usual banter inside the stadium, including many renditions of '99 Soccer Reds' from the ASC. Raymie was there and it must have brought back some pretty grim memories for him. But apart from the usual pleasantries nothing went off.

It was a different story after the game. We had concealed ourselves in every vantage point we could find and when Aberdeen reached London Road we attacked. Only this time we were smarter. Instead of steaming into the head of their mob, where the top boys were waiting, we ran into the middle where the less confident guys tended to position themselves. It not only confused them but also stopped their vanguard from building up a head of steam. Another important difference was that we were well mobbed up with, I estimate, about five hundred boys.

The battle raged all the way back to Waverley, with the two sides going at it hammer and tongs. A building site was raided and we launched into each other with bricks, scaffolding poles and pieces of wood. Both mobs had by this time split into two groups and we forced one lot of ASC to retreat into the station through the side entrance. We then turned our attention to the other side of Princes Street, where the rest of their mob was preparing to take on the other group of CCS. Hostilities recommenced, with neither side prepared to back off. Meanwhile the ASC who had been run into the station had not boarded a train for Aberdeen as we hoped. Looking to get back into the fight they came straight up the ramp at the front entrance to Waverley and reappeared on Princes Street. This was going to be a long, gruelling battle.

It was time to play our joker.

One of the Hibs Baby Crew took the bull by the horns, or should I say the bottle by the neck. He lit the rag and hurled that fucker right into a group of Aberdeen boys.

Whoosh!

I watched open-mouthed as a Molotov cocktail flew through the air and smashed onto the pavement outside the Wimpey bar. Flames erupted, scattering not only the ASC but also crowds of passers-by, who go the fright of their lives. There was chaos. Dozens of people spilled onto Princes Street. Women were crying, children screaming. Their boys, not knowing if we had more bombs, ran for their lives. I also legged it, ending up in St Andrew's Square, where the police stopped me and some other CCS. They sniffed our arms for petrol, found nothing and sent us on our way.

The operation then took what could have been an even more dangerous turn. After the cops had let me go I made immediately for Princes Street Gardens with a pal. We had hidden a stash of petrol bombs alongside the railway line. Our plan was to smash the windows of Aberdeen's train and throw the bombs right into the carriages. If we had succeeded there would have been serious injuries to dozens, perhaps hundreds, of people. I can't guarantee that innocent passengers would not have been hurt but that wasn't our intention. It was strictly personal between us and the ASC. Some people will take the view that what we planned to do was extreme but it shows how bent on revenge we were. But, as they say, the best laid plans. When we got to our cache we discovered that the cops must have got there first and taken the petrol bombs away. Then we were stopped by two of Edinburgh's finest, who asked us what we were doing there and why our hands were so dirty. They thought it was from handling petrol but we told them they got that way because we had jumped over the turnstiles and they let us go.

In the pub that night we were ecstatic, wired to the moon. Where Aberdeen were concerned we had got our own back in the most spectacular way possible.[3] The only cloud on the horizon was that the cops arrested the Baby Crew member who had thrown the bomb, but, fortunately, he was found either not guilty or not proven at his trial and walked free from the court. There was also an important spin-off from the afternoon's events: as a mob the CCS had been strengthened because many of the boys who had fronted up for the ASC had had their appetites whetted and wanted more. And, more importantly, we had put down a marker to every other mob in Scotland and beyond: we were prepared to do whatever it took to win. There would be no stopping us now.

Although we were now well on the way to being number one in

---

[3] Aberdeen were shocked by the petrol bomb. In the other book written by an ASC member, (*Congratulations: You Have Just Met the Casuals* by Dan Rivers, London 2005) the author notes 'If I'm honest I got a scare . . . . It seemed like the game had turned into guerrilla warfare and that wasn't what it was about for me.' Again, fair enough, Dan but your fellow gang members shouldn't have kicked someone half to death and then bragged about it. The papers were, as you would expect, full of the story. The *Sunday Mail* of 13 October 1985 reported that 'A petrol bomber brought terror to a Scots city . . . the bomb . . . sent people fleeing in terror when it exploded on the Waverley Steps.'

ABERDEEN: JUST A GOOD, HONEST MOB

Scotland Aberdeen were, and would remain, the best of the rest. They tried to get back at us in November 1985 at Hampden, just a few weeks after the petrol-bomb incident, when the two clubs met in the League Cup final. There were about six hundred on each side that day and it would have been one of the biggest battles in hooligan history. The only problem was the Glasgow police got a firm handle on the situation and kept the two mobs apart.

Aberdeen tried again at Easter Road in January 1986. The main part of the away end, at that time open terracing, was closed due to heavy snow and so Aberdeen were herded into the standing enclosure. We saw an opportunity and began to pile into the enclosure. Although about twenty made it the cops, hearing our accents, soon got wise to the ploy and refused to let any more of us in. But there were still enough CCS to cause a problem. It kicked off from a quite unexpected source. Someone ran out from the Aberdeen group and shouted:

'I am Crazy Legs. I am Millwall.'

Not to be outdone Sean Welsh replied:

'I am Sean Welsh. I am Hibs.'

With that Sean punched Crazy Legs full in the kisser, which sparked off a short but quite satisfying fight that ended with the bizzies throwing everyone with an Edinburgh accent out of the enclosure.

We had many a memorable set to with them, none more thrilling than in Dundee before a Scottish Cup semi-final on 5 April 1986. We took about three hundred to the game and I think Aberdeen had about the same. We had missed each other at the railway station, by accident not design, but after that there were running battles all over Dundee city centre as the two mobs fragmented into smaller groups. I remember battling in pubs, in shops and in the middle of the road. I ended up in a children's play park, in a quite superb fifty-a-side confrontation. It was just two great mobs going at it with no quarter either asked for or granted. To me it was one of the best days in the annals of hooliganism, a true clash of the titans.

Aberdeen considered themselves invulnerable at home, but we more than held our own up there. In November 1987 we went up to Pittodrie for a midweek game with an evening kick off. The buses were parked near to a funfair and we walked to the top of the hill that overlooks the stadium. When the ASC spotted us we charged. It was a particularly intense fight, with a few dozen on each side. I certainly remember landing many punches and kicks. Although we did not, as a general rule, carry knives one ASC fighter was stabbed by one of our lot, a boy we had nicknamed 'Dodgy D'. I am led to believe that the Aberdeen casual only survived because he was wearing several layers of clothing. Dodgy D was wearing a black leather jacket that night so the Bill arrested every Hibs boy who happened to be wearing one but they got no joy.

The next week, the Aberdeen polis turned up at Easter Road, determined to catch the guilty party. The cops forced an ASC member who had witnessed the stabbing to go with them but it was the day that Celtic infamously threw a CS gas canister into the Hibs end and the place was in uproar. With a major tragedy a strong possibility it was neither the time nor the place to look for a suspect. In any event the Aberdeen lad had no intention of fingering Dodgy D (who is now, sadly, deceased). The Aberdeen cops went home empty handed.

In those days, the mid to late Eighties, it seemed that something major went down every time we faced Aberdeen and another midweek fixture in May 1988, also at Pittodrie, was quite outstanding. We travelled north in a convoy of cars and a minibus. Nothing happened before or during the game and after we left the stadium we headed for a pub in Union Street, Aberdeen's main thoroughfare. We kept our heads down, giving the impression that we were just a group of lads out for a quiet drink. Our reasoning was that the cops would think we had called it a night and headed back to Edinburgh. If it worked it meant we could attack Aberdeen without being rudely interrupted. After an hour or so we ventured out, got into our vehicles and went looking for the ASC. We knew they frequented a pub just off Union Street and sure enough the boys in the minibus, which had got separated from the cars, saw a couple of their boys going into the pub. Bingo!

But our minibus had been spotted and they immediately put two and two together. Their whole crew rushed out of the pub and helped themselves to bricks, metal poles and lumps of wood from a builder's skip. Seeing only the lads in the minibus the ASC thought they were onto a winner. A volley of bricks – and, strangely enough, a sandwich board – was launched at the minibus and shattered the windscreen. The CCS boys jumped out and although they were heavily outnumbered immediately ran towards Aberdeen. Then about thirty seconds later the cars arrived with passengers that included Girvan, Kev Wood, Mikey Neri, Horan and me. The minibus contingent included Taylor, Bobby Lipscombe and Keek, all game boys. As usual we weren't tooled up, but when we saw what Aberdeen were holding we realised immediately that we had to fight fire with fire. The car boots were opened and we armed ourselves with hammers, screwdrivers, wheel jacks and torches. What followed was brutal and I have to say that we ran riot. The ASC seemed to go into a state of shock when the cars pulled up and they never recovered. I had a 'black pudding' (a long Maglite torch) and I well remember laying into one of their boys in a shop doorway. I bet he had a sore head in the morning.

These are only a few of the scraps we had with Aberdeen. In fact we have probably fought them more than any other mob in Scotland, with both sides winning and losing their fair share. That is no doubt why I got to know so many of their top guys so well, guys like Ray, Monkey and Weg. I respect them. They are all good, honest boys who would rather throw a punch than pull a knife. We became so close that we even ended up helping each other out. One time Ray and a few of the ASC were in Edinburgh for a trial in the sheriff court. We heard about it and decided to look for them at Waverley. It wasn't a social call; we had mayhem on our minds. But when we got there we discovered that Ray's pals had caught an earlier train and he was alone in the station. Apart from liking the guy I felt it was cowardly for a mob to attack someone who was on his own. I persuaded my pals to let him go on his way unmolested. He later returned the favour when I was on up a charge in Aberdeen sheriff court. Helping out the members of another mob is considered heresy by some of my CCS colleagues. I like to think of it as professional courtesy.

Nowadays I talk regularly to current and former ASC members on the phone, reminiscing, recalling shared memories, getting nostalgic. I know that they, like me, would give anything for the great days to come back, for us to be going toe to toe outside Pittodrie or chasing each other down Easter Road.

8
THE KRONK: THE ROAD TO WAR

I had no choice but to attack the Kronk that night in September 1990. I had been pushed to the limits of my endurance and I snapped. Simple as that. There was no other way. I had been put through hell by my enemies; they had even threatened my family. Some people will say that I should have gone to the police but that would have done no good. Somewhere, somehow I would have been taken out; they might even have torched my house. And with a wife and two kids that was a chance I just couldn't take.

The consequences of my actions that night were severe. I became embroiled in the longest trial in Scottish criminal history at that time, a trial marked by violence, witness intimidation, jury tampering and levels of courtroom security not seen outside of Belfast when there are half a dozen IRA men in the dock. I became a fugitive from justice, spending weeks on the run. My personal life was turned upside down. I forfeited valuable contracts to manage doors. My marriage crumbled. I lost contact with my sons during their formative years. I brought shame on my family. I became known as the 'axe-man thug' in the media. Some of my friends, there to support me, were arrested and they also faced a High Court trial.

And then there is the small matter of a five-year prison sentence for attempted murder.

The Kronk wasn't a place. It wasn't even a building. It was the name of a rave organised by casuals, and it was held in a Dunfermline pub called the Well. But what happened there has gone down in hooligan history. It was by some distance the most extreme incident involving casuals that has ever taken place in Scotland, perhaps even in Britain. I laugh when I watch the film *Cass*, which is about the West Ham boy, Cass Pennant. In the movie we see Pennant and his mates launch an organised assault on Newcastle fans in a working-men's club. The film makes out that it was one of the most notorious acts ever perpetrated by casuals. Maybe it was but it pales into insignificance compared to what happened that night at the Kronk. This is not bravado or the idle boasting of a middle-aged thug whose best fighting days are behind him. I am simply stating a fact.

The roots of such savage battles normally run deep and the Kronk was no exception to the rule. In fact they went back for a decade or more and involved a number of gangs and different factions. But I would say there were two main causes. The first was that I was a Hibs boy living in Fife. That irritated Dunfermline's Carnegie Soccer Service (the CSS), who probably thought I should be supporting their team. The second factor was the non-football rivalry between Dunfermline and my home towns of Rosyth, where I was brought up, and Inverkeithing, just two miles down the road, my marital home after moving back to Fife from Edinburgh in 1986. It meant that I was taking a huge gamble any time I ventured into Dunfermline. With the majority of the CCS being resident in Edinburgh I would have to take on the CSS either on my own or with the assistance of a few volunteers from Inverkeithing and Rosyth.

Two incidents from that period epitomise what I was up against. One afternoon in the late 1980s I had been out on a shoplifting expedition in Dunfermline town centre with a mate. After a successful day we decided to call it quits and to go back to our car with the ill-gotten gains. On the way we ran into four Dunfermline and as we went past they barged right into us. We couldn't do much about it at the time: we had stolen goods concealed beneath our jackets and stuffed down our trousers. So when we got to the car we dumped the goods and went back to look for them. There was a confrontation in which angry words were exchanged, but it didn't come to blows. Believing that a fight was off the agenda I turned and walked away.

The next thing I remember was waking up in hospital. One of the CSS had hit me when my back was turned, knocking me to the ground. It was when I fell that the damage was done. My head hit one of those ornamental flower pots and knocked me clean out.

On another occasion, around the same time, four of us went to a Dunfermline nightclub and were standing having a drink in the VIP area. We could see there were quite a number of CSS in the club and I just had a sixth sense that something was going to happen. They bided their time until two of our group went to the toilet and, seizing their opportunity, about fifteen of them set about us. As a Hibs boy I was their main target and I still have the scars to prove it. There is one on the right side of my head, the result of being struck by a Grolsch bottle. The other scar is on the left side of my head and was put there by a glass tumbler. I was semi-conscious, saturated in my own blood and had to be rushed to hospital in an ambulance. That night I was wearing a white shirt but the nurses actually thought it was a red one when they took it off, simply because of the amount of blood it had absorbed.

Another source of conflict was the enmity between Dunfermline and Inverkeithing/Rosyth, which was not really football-related, more the natural rivalry between towns that sit almost cheek by jowl. I had of course been active in that feud in my teenage years and had been sent to detention centre for my part in two nights of rioting. Now that I was back in Inverkeithing I often got involved, at other times I was too busy fighting with the CCS. But whether I was there or not the fights between the two gangs ratcheted up the tension a few more notches.

The most notorious encounter took place at Inverkeithing railway station in the late 1980s. Inverkeithing had its own little gang, the Divit Station Trendies[4], and its main aim in life was to inflict as much punishment on the CSS as possible. A prime opportunity arose when Dunfermline were playing at Dundee and had to change trains on the way home at, of all places, Inverkeithing. The Divit boys had been planning all week for the Saturday and had gathered dozens of bottles, bricks and planks of wood, which they hid next to a petrol station just

---

[4] Divit is a nickname for Inverkeithing, but don't ask me why.

a stone's throw from the station. Their planning worked. When Dunfermline got off the train the sixty or so DST ran down the road onto the platform and pelted the CSS with the missiles they had collected. There was only one cop there at the time and he had no chance of keeping the two sides apart. The battle raged for about ten minutes and I believe the home mob gave their opponents a real kicking, one that they still boast about to this day. It was only the arrival of police reinforcements that saved Dunfermline from even more serious injury. One DST boy wasn't so lucky. He was nicked and got six months for his pains.

I wasn't at the station. In fact I was fighting Hearts that day and had been arrested and taken to a nick in Edinburgh. But that didn't stop the cops from trying to implicate me in the attack on Dunfermline. I was apprehended on the Sunday at my house and taken to a cop shop. The whole thing was a farce and it proved once again, at least in my eyes, what corrupt bastards many cops are. I can well remember the questions they asked;

'How is it that none of them [the DST] will stick you in for the railway-station attack?' I was asked.

'Because I wasn't fucking there.'

'Well, we have an eye-witness who saw you there.'

'He must be mistaken.'

'He is not mistaken. He is 100 per cent sure it was you. So we are going to caution you and put you through a question-and-answer session.'

I could of course have told them about what had happened in Edinburgh but I wanted to get into court and expose them for the stupid, lying bastards they are. Although I did eventually tell them that I had been arrested at the football – which they verified with their colleagues in Edinburgh – there is no doubt in my mind that charges would have brought against me for the railway-station incident if it hadn't been for my watertight alibi. So don't talk to me about police integrity. In my experience they will do anything to get a conviction no matter how many innocent victims get in their way. I was slung out of the cop shop without an apology and the bastards didn't even give me a lift home.

The attack at the station was a further fanning of the flames between the Dunfermline boys and Inverkeithing. There were also flashpoints that arose from my membership of the CCS. These flashpoints often arose when I was travelling to and from Fife, simply because I would be on my own or at best with a couple of pals. There was a good example in 1986 after we played Celtic, when I got the train home from Waverley with two other boys from Inverkeithing. We were soon joined by eight Dunfermline casuals and got into a discussion with them about who had the best mob. They argued for Celtic, we insisted it was Hibs. The conversation was light-hearted at first, like a friendly argument. Then it got heated. I made the point that Celtic had never done Hibs and never would. That pissed them off and one of them whispered to his pal:

'We've never done Hibs. Let's fucking do it now.'

We weren't meant to hear the comment but fortunately I had. That gave me time to roll up the newspaper I was carrying into a 'Millwall Brick', so called because it feels like a brick when you are hit. When they made their move I punched the one nearest me with the Brick, bursting his nose wide open. His mates then got stuck in and seeing that the odds were stacked against us my two companions chickened out, dived into the toilet and locked the door. I was left to face eight Dunfermline on my own. Under normal circumstances I would have got a hiding but being on the train saved my bacon. I had my back to the carriage door, which meant there was only room for one or two of them to attack me at any one time. I lashed out with my feet and even managed to clobber a couple more with the Brick. This lasted for a few minutes until the train pulled into Inverkeithing, where the three of us got off.

Although the Dunfermline boys stayed on the train I had a fair idea there would be retribution. It came the very next night in Inverkeithing. In the company of two pals I was walking my elder son in his buggy when three cars drew up and about twelve of them got out. Before they could surround us I shouted on one of the boys with me to run to the pub and get reinforcements. Then I turned my attention to the baying mob that was confronting us. I had had the foresight to arm myself with a hammer, which was in a plastic shopping bag hanging from the handles of the baby buggy. It was just as well: my pal, Jamie, had been punched to the ground and was getting his head kicked in. I knew I had to do something to protect him and so I grabbed that bag and started swinging it at them for all I was worth. They knew there was something heavy and hard in the bag and started to back off. In fact, by the time reinforcements arrived from the pub they were back in their cars and taking off for Dunfermline.

Just a few months later we were at it again, although on this occasion the initial contact was simply a coincidence. Along with my brother and my son I had taken a bus from Inverkeithing to the garden centre at Dalgety Bay, a distance of less than three miles. We were on the lower deck and throughout the journey there was constant singing, clapping and stamping of feet from upstairs. When we got off the bus we discovered what all the fuss was about. It was Dunfermline. They had seen me get on and were warming up for another crack. As my brother and I manoeuvred the pram off the bus they spat on us and threw coins. I was livid. I had my infant son with me and he could have been seriously hurt.

I abandoned the visit to the garden centre and took a taxi back to Inverkeithing. When I got home I made a few quick calls to members of the Divit Station Trendies and put together a little mob. We knew Dunfermline would have to come back through Inverkeithing on their way home. All we had to do was wait.

Sure enough, after about two hours, the bus came into view. When it reached the stop on High Street I jumped on and, with my anger now at boiling point, ran up the stairs. Lifting one of the bench seats out of its frame I set about the Dunfermline boys and landed a few heavy blows with the seat. At the same time my Divit Station pals were smashing the bus windows with bricks and stones. With my point made I decided to leg it before the Old Bill arrived and fairly sprinted down the stairs. One of their boys threw a brick at the back of my head but missed. The poor old bus driver wasn't so lucky. The brick hit him on the crown, knocking him unconscious. The police did arrive and although I managed to evade arrest they caught up with me a few days later. I was charged with assault but walked away from court with a not guilty. It seems that some of the witnesses just couldn't remember what actually happened. I wonder why.

There were many more confrontations with the Dunfermline mob after that. I was always going to be a target. Fair enough. It went with the territory and it was something I could live with. But for their part it was so much more personal. They just could not accept that a Hibs boy was living in their midst; it seemed to enrage them that a Fifer, one of their own, was a leading player in another mob. They had put me in hospital twice and were no doubt just waiting for the right opportunity to make it a hat trick. They did get another opportunity but this time they messed it up. This time they targeted my wife and family, something that no one on this earth is going to get away with.

Strangely enough the incident that would lead directly to the attack on the Kronk came about as we were preparing to take on another mob, a mob that operated four hundred miles away, in London. It was August 1990 and Hibs were due to play Millwall in a Friday-night friendly. We had hired two buses to take us south but as we were preparing to leave Edinburgh late on the Thursday night the cops came into the pub and told us they had found out about our plan and had sent the buses away. We were still determined to get to London, and we decided to go home and to travel down by train or car the next day.

I went back to Inverkeithing with Horan, one of my best pals in the mob. We got there about midnight and decided to call in at Captain Jack's, a pub with a nightclub attached, where I worked as a doorman. It was well known in the area that the CCS was going down to Millwall and so the pub and the nightclub, in our absence, were full of Dunfermline boys. When we walked in you could have heard the proverbial pin drop. It was like a scene from one of those Westerns where the sheriff and his deputy walk into a saloon full of desperadoes. Despite eying each other warily for the rest of the night nothing went off but at closing time they lined up outside, about thirty of them, waiting for Horan and I to emerge.

We decided to get our retaliation in first.

Horan scooped up as many bottles and glasses as he could carry and I did the same. We charged out of the doors and let fly with a volley of glass. There were some handy Inverkeithing guys there that night and they were a big help, as was one of the guys on the door. I reckon that made it eleven of us in all but despite being outnumbered we ended up chasing them along the road. Some of them went past us in a car, which a group of us proceeded to smash up. When the car got through our group they got out and opened the boot, which had quite an array of weapons in it, including baseball bats, knives and screwdrivers. It all kicked off again and one of them hit me with a lump of wood, which left an L-shaped scar on my face. But once again we got the better of it and gave them a right kicking. There was a comical moment when one of their boys was climbing metal railings but got caught by his hood. As he was hanging there, rather forlornly, we laid into him with sticks.

The police arrived but we told them we were just interested spectators to what had gone on. They had no option but to accept our explanation and we headed back to Captain Jack's for a final drink. By now it was half three in the morning and we had a train to catch to London in three hours' time. Just time for a quick trip home and a shower before heading to Waverley and so Horan and I cadged a lift from two of the doormen. It had been a job well done, something we could entertain the other CCS boys with on the long journey south. As we turned into my street my thoughts were turning to Millwall and the challenges that lay ahead. So I got the shock of my life when I saw that my house was completely surrounded by Dunfermline. When we drew up they swarmed round the car and as we tried to get out they were lashing out with bricks, stones and lumps of wood. The driver reversed, knocking over a few of them in the process, and he managed to manoeuvre the car over some waste ground and get away. My intention was to round up a few boys and to go back and sort them out, but by that time everyone had gone to bed.

I still went to Millwall and when I told the rest of the boys that Dunfermline had come to my house they were livid. That wasn't what casuals did. We fought each other, on neutral territory, not outside our houses where wives, girlfriends and children were sleeping. Fuck that shit. They were also well aware that Dunfermline had twice put me in hospital. It was unthinkable that such a thing could happen to a member of Scotland's leading firm, especially at the hands of such a crap mob. The boys all said they would come up to Fife any time I asked. They wanted to teach the cunts a lesson they would never forget.

When I got back from Millwall the pressure from Dunfermline, if anything, intensified. Although we eventually managed to get our phone number classified as ex-directory for a period of time it seemed to be known to all and sundry. We got anonymous phone calls twenty-four/seven. The content of the calls was always along these lines:

'You're fucking getting it. You're dead. We're coming to petrol bomb your house.'

I tried to psyche them out, to get them to tell me where they were or to goad them into coming to the house when I was sure to be there:

'You obviously know where I stay so come doon and fucking dae it. I'm in the house just now. You know where I am so why don't you tell me where you are. Don't be a fucking coward and hide behind anonymity.'

But of course they wouldn't tell me who they were. Margo took most of the calls, including some from people threatening to harm our two sons, so you can imagine what kind of state she was in. She was already worried to death about my life with the casuals and the consequences for us as a family. It can't be very pleasant fretting about your husband being hospitalised every Saturday or having your door kicked in by burly polis looking to make an arrest. Now her children were being threatened and that is something no mother can tolerate. We rowed constantly about it. For our peace of mind something had to be done. But what precisely? I immediately ruled out going to the police. With my record I doubt if I would have got any sympathy, much less a cop car outside the house. And even if I had involved them it wouldn't have changed a thing. The Dunfermline boys would still have come after me. There was just too much bad blood for it to stop. There would have to be a day of reckoning.

It was a job for the CCS.

9
THE KRONK: THE ATTACK

Despite our natural inclination to go after Dunfermline immediately we decided to play it cool. To lull them into a false sense of security. There is a saying that revenge is a dish best served cold. That was our view. But that doesn't mean we were idle. We used the time to plan, to prepare, to work out how, when and where to strike. We knew that their favourite haunt was the Well, a pub in the Rumblingwell area of Dunfermline. The Well also had a function room, which was used among other things for a rave night that was known as the Kronk.[5] The Kronk was run by the Dunfermline casuals: they printed the tickets, booked the DJ, provided the security. The place was always full of CSS, their women and their hangers-on. It was a target-rich environment.

So our first move was to case the Well to find out where the doors and emergency exits were, and how long it would take us to drive from there back to Captain Jack's in Inverkeithing. We wanted to give ourselves a cast-iron alibi. If I could get back to Captain Jack's and put on my doorman's suit before the cops turned up I could make the claim that I had never been anywhere near Dunfermline. I had many friends and sympathisers among the Captain Jack's clientele and was sure they

---

[5] It was named after the famous boxing gym in Detroit. Run by the legendary trainer, Emanuel Steward, the Kronk produced many world champions including Thomas 'the Hit Man' Hearns.

would back me up. In the meantime the other boys would either have high-tailed it back to Edinburgh or melted into the nightclub throng.

Three weeks after the CSS came to my house we made our move. It was a Friday night – 7 September 1990 to be precise – and we knew the Kronk would be heaving with Dunfermline. It was the ideal opportunity not just to get a bit of vengeance but also to wreak real havoc, to give them a beating they would never forget, a beating that would perhaps even finish them as a mob. We were certainly up to the task. We had been at the game for five years and had experienced the best that Britain had to offer. A second-rate firm like Dunfermline wasn't going to stand in our way.

Thirty of our boys made the short journey across from Edinburgh, every one of them a battle-hardened thug. We had also recruited five drivers, all from the Rosyth and Inverkeithing area. Their knowledge of the local roads would be vital if we were to get back to Captain Jack's before the police got on our tail. We were also well tooled-up. That was not the normal CCS practice but we knew Dunfermline almost always carried weapons and would not hesitate to use them. Some of our boys had knives, others baseball bats, still others iron bars. One guy had a sword while I was carrying an axe. I wasn't intending to kill anyone so I made a conscious decision to leave the leather cover on the blade.

It is difficult to convey the atmosphere inside the car that night. Of course my primary emotion was gratitude. The boys were taking a hell of a risk for me and I was so grateful for their support. And yes we were apprehensive, not just about what would happen when we got there but also about the reaction of the criminal-justice system. If we were caught we would be facing serious jail time. But there was a much stronger emotion, one that overwhelmed everything else. It was pride. I felt proud, proud that we were going into battle as a united mob. We were in this together; we would look out for each other. We would prevail.

Let battle commence.

We got to Dunfermline just after eleven, parking the five cars in William Street, just a stone's throw from the Well. The drivers stayed in the vehicles and the engines were left running to ensure a quick getaway. We put on balaclavas and hooded jackets, piled out and smashed right through the front door. Our next stop was the function room, where the Kronk rave was in full swing. It was at this point that our plan started to go awry. The bouncers must have seen us coming and had barricaded the entrance door seconds before we got there. We did our best to kick it down but we just couldn't get the fucking thing to budge.

It was time for Plan B.

We went back outside and found the side door, which took us into the public bar. Once inside we picked up bottles and glasses and did our best to smash the place up. But as our main aim was to get into the Kronk we moved quickly towards the alternative entrance to the function room. Some smart cunt wanted to play the hero and he stood right in front us, blocking our path. There's always one. We took him out with a few well-aimed blows and turned our attention to the door. Once again we couldn't break it down. It had been well and truly fortified with tables and chairs by the Kronk's patrons and there was just no way through. Plan B was quickly abandoned and we now moved on to Plan C.

We went back out through the side door and made our way to the fire door at the back of the function room. It was also locked so we picked up a beer keg and hurled it at the glazed section of the door, which shattered into a thousand pieces. One of the boys leaned over the open half of the door and tried to release the lock, but no joy. We had to content ourselves with throwing bricks through the door at the guys inside and they responded in kind. By this time the place was in uproar. Although the music had been switched off since we attacked the decibel level had if anything increased. There were around two hundred people at the rave, half of them women who had been ingesting Ecstasy all night, and the shouting and screaming, combined with the sound of breaking glass, made the noise deafening.

Then we got the break we needed. Our new plan, Plan D, was to make a second attempt at gaining entry via the front door. So we sprinted round there and as we were running we were met head on by twenty Dunfermline. They had decided to come out of hiding and to run round the outside of the building and surprise us. There was no time to think or for anyone to back out. We had collided head on and there was nothing else for it but to engage. They were well armed with pool cues, glasses and bottles but faced with a mob of our calibre they had little chance. Within seconds one of them was badly cut by our swordsman. Several more were pummelled by baseball bats. One guy was hit by a chair before being stabbed in the shoulder. And when one of their boys, to his credit, put up a real fight he was clubbed to the ground and savagely beaten by four of us. It was a massacre and quite understandably they bottled out and started to run.

I was in the thick of the action and hit my immediate opponent with the sharp end of the axe. As the blow landed there was a dull thud. I will never forget his scream. It was so loud that it drowned out all the shouting and swearing and general commotion around us. He staggered but stayed on his feet and tried to get away. Then he was struck at least twenty more times by my fellow CCS. Finally, I caught him with a powerful blow to the shoulder and this time he did go down. In my anger I had hit him far harder than I intended. His whole back had opened up and I understand that when the cops arrived two of them had to hold it together until the ambulance got there. I also discovered that a woman police officer fainted when she saw the injuries he had sustained.

The Dunfermline boys who got away from us managed to get back inside the pub and to barricade the front door. It was time for us to go. We had done our jobs and it would only be a matter of minutes before the bizzies were on the scene. Then, to our surprise, Dunfermline reappeared. They must have swallowed a dose of bravery pills. As we departed the scene they were steaming out of the Well and mouthing off about what they were going to do to us. One of our guys took the bait and ran into them. But there was no time for any more and we dragged him away before he got us all nicked. It was a good decision. Just as we pulled out of William Street police cars arrived from all directions, sirens blaring. But we were away.

Two of our cars headed for the Kincardine Bridge. The reasoning was that the police would have put roadblocks on the Forth Road Bridge, which was in any event easier to control because at that time the toll regime was still in place. Good choice. The Old Bill did roadblock the

Forth crossing so the ten boys in those two cars got back to Edinburgh without any hassle. The rest of us headed for Captain Jack's where I quickly donned my monkey suit and went out front, pretending for all the world that nothing untoward had happened. A few minutes later I was called to the phone to speak to a pal and as I was chatting I became aware of three pairs of size-ten black boots out of the corner of my eye. It hadn't taken them long to get here and when I got off the phone the questioning started. I knew one of the cops and he did most of the talking.

'Can I have a word with you, Andy?' he asked.

'Aye.'

'There's been an incident up at the Well tonight. Guys fighting, serious injuries and the place got smashed up.'

'Aye. I know.'

He was taken aback by my answer and said:

'How did you know about it?'

'Well a couple of the taxi drivers were in earlier and warned us that a gang from Edinburgh was in Dunfermline smashing up pubs. They were tipping us off that they might come here.'

'The problem is that you have been implicated in it,' he insisted.

'Dinnae be daft. I have been standing here working all night as you can see.'

'Aye that's as maybe but we'll have to speak to you. Do you mind having a seat in the back of the car?' he asked, very politely.

'As a matter of fact I do. I'm no' daft. Once I'm in the car I'll be whisked off to the station. It's happened to me before.'

'Well we've got orders from our sergeant to bring you in so let's go.'

With that I started to walk up the stairs to the bar, where my wife was working. The cop who had done all the talking was unhappy with that and he asked:

'Where do think you're going?'

'Well if you're taking me to the police station I have to tell my wife where I'm going.'

'Okay then, but come straight back down when you have spoken to her.'

When I got to the top of the stairs I saw Horan, grabbed him by the arm and pointed him in the direction of the fire exit. We pushed open the door, walked down the stairs and ran along the railway line.

I was on the run.

10
THE KRONK: PAYING THE PRICE

I knew that despite our elaborate planning there was a good chance I would be in the frame for the Kronk. There was too much history between me and the Dunfermline boys, a history that the police were only too well aware of. But I never contemplated going on the run. It was a crazy, spur-of-the-moment decision taken when the cops came to arrest me at Captain Jack's. I don't know what was in my mind. Perhaps it was the adrenaline still coursing through my veins that spurred me on.

After slipping down the fire exit at Captain Jack's we ran along the railway line and headed for the flat of a girl I knew. She had been half expecting us; her flatmate's boyfriend was a Dunfermline casual and had phoned to tell her about what happened that night.[6] Once safely inside I phoned one of my CCS mates and asked him to come over from Edinburgh and pick us up when the coast was clear. The Old Bill had been searching cars at the Forth Road Bridge and we knew we would have to wait until they decided to abandon that operation. The next day, we got the call. The bridge was clear and so the afternoon after the attack we drove to a safe house in Niddrie, a council estate in the east of the city.

---

[6] The flatmate would later give evidence against us. She saw my pal wipe blood off his shoes and was able to testify to that effect.

I alternated between Niddrie and houses on the south side of Edinburgh and soon discovered that after the initial excitement being a fugitive from justice is just about the most monotonous existence known to man. It is almost as bad as the jail. Going anywhere is a risk and when you do you are always looking over your shoulder. I did manage to go to Celtic Park to watch Hibs but I had to don a hat and scarf to make me look like a normal fan. It was essential to keep a low profile and so there was no chance of getting involved in any fights, which for me was like going cold turkey. I also hated staying in other people's houses, even if I did appreciate the risk my friends were taking in hiding me. We all like to be masters of our own domain and that is impossible when you are crashing out on a living-room couch.

I wasn't on the run for long, about three weeks in fact. One day I had been in the centre of Edinburgh and caught a bus to Leith to meet up with some CCS pals. I jumped off the bus and we were walking along Pilrig Street when a line of cars, driving in what seemed like a convoy, went past. If I had clocked them at all I would probably have concluded they had been at a funeral. I would have been right.

There was only one problem. It was a police funeral.

There had been a huge turnout of Old Bill that day for a deceased bizzie and this was them either on the way back to the station or en route to the wake. They were driving their own cars and not marked vehicles, which, of course, meant I was off guard. To make it even worse one of the filth was the football-intelligence specialist for Hibs. He had spotted me and I watched open-mouthed as his car performed an emergency U-turn. It then accelerated violently and screeched to a halt about two feet from where we were standing. A couple of seconds later a second car drew up behind us and four or five of the bastards surrounded me and stuck the cuffs on. It was a stroke of bad luck and I thought I would be shattered but to be honest my overwhelming emotion was relief. Knowing that one day you are going to get lifted, but not knowing exactly when that might be, is very stressful.

I was taken to Constitution Street station in Leith. They contacted Fife police and an hour later two CID officers arrived and escorted me to Dunfermline cop shop, where I was fingerprinted and charged with mobbing and rioting and attempted murder. The next morning I was hauled in front of Dunfermline sheriff court on what is known as 'petition'. I was not asked to plead either guilty or not guilty and was bailed to reappear in court at a later date.

Given the number of people likely to be involved and the fact that it was to be held in the High Court, Scotland's most senior criminal court, I knew that I would be waiting for months. Once you have been charged they have a year and a day to try you, which gives them plenty of time to prepare. I had no doubt what the eventual outcome would be: they were out to get me and when the establishment is in that mood there is nothing you can do. Think of the song: 'I fought the law and the law won'. It would have made no difference if I had behaved myself or not in the pre-trial period; I was going down and I was going down big time.

With a long prison sentence ahead I decided to make the most of life. I threw myself into the hooligan scene with renewed vigour and we had some memorable battles in that period. I was arrested twice and on one of those occasions, in May 1991, after a fight in Perth with St Johnstone fans, I was charged with breach of the peace and assault. I had to plead guilty because if I had opted for not guilty my bail for the Kronk would have been revoked and I would have been back inside on remand. The Perth incident landed me with a fine but it was better than being in a prison cell for months on end.

Then, almost a year after the raid on the Kronk, came the day of reckoning. I doubt if there has ever been a trial like it, either before or since. At the time it was the longest ever held in the High Court, starting on 1 July 1991 and lasting until 2 August 1991. However, given that there were four accused and more than 150 witnesses that length of time was necessary. Another feature was the security precautions, which were unprecedented. In fact the only thing I can compare them to is a major IRA trial at the Old Bailey. Quite clearly the powers-that-be were worried: about witness and juror intimidation; about the CCS running riot; even about an attempt to spring me and my fellow accused.

They must have spent a fortune. To keep an eye on my CCS pals cameras were installed inside Dunfermline High Court, a practice that is now commonplace but very rare eighteen years ago. Outside the police station there is a big roundabout on which the bizzies erected a pole and stuck a camera on the top. It was powerful enough to sweep the whole town centre including the bus and railway stations and the court buildings. Another huge camera was positioned on top of the multi-storey car park, which perches above the bus station. The boys couldn't pick their fucking noses without plod knowing about it.

The security precautions for transporting us to and from Saughton prison in Edinburgh were even more elaborate. Although I was out on bail for much of the trial a decision was taken to remand me at the end of the Crown evidence and I was held in Saughton. There were always three police cars in the convoy. I was in one with two big polis sat next to me and then there was a car in front of us and one behind, all with their sirens blaring at full volume. We were also flanked by two motorcycle outriders. Fair enough but what I didn't expect was that they would close off the motorway slip roads and junctions along the way until we had passed safely. I accept that security is important but this was way over the top.

Then there was my very own personal-security detail. For the early part of the trial two cops followed me everywhere, keeping about six feet behind. There was no attempt to hide it. If I walked down the street and went into a shop they waited at the door until I came out. At lunch time during the court case I would go down to the Glen, a big park in Dunfermline, with my then girlfriend and her baby daughter to enjoy the sunshine and have a bit of lunch. We would be sitting on one park bench with the baby buggy in front of us and the two bizzies would be sat on the bench opposite. They even went to the same bakery to buy sandwiches!

Although the security was at times over the top I have to admit that some of the measures taken were, from the point of view of the police, essential. Because there is no denying there was widespread witness and juror intimidation throughout the trial. The CCS were desperate to get us off and the boys did their level best to make witnesses keep their mouths shut. In the first instance they tried friendly persuasion, getting people to see reason, and if that didn't work they were threatened with violence. I understand that while some were dealt with a later date others got theirs on the spot.

Perhaps the best example was the day the boys got a phone call to say that some Dunfermline casuals were in a petrol station in Rosyth. They jumped in the car, rushed round and confronted them on the forecourt, warning them about not giving evidence. To emphasise the point one of the boys pulled out a knife and stabbed a Dunfermline casual up the arse. 'That's what you'll all fucking get if you give evidence against us,' he told them.

There was another key witness for the prosecution, who worked as a hairdresser in Edinburgh. He got regular visits from the CCS warning him about the consequences of testifying. In another incident a member of the CCS was charged with running down a Crown witness with his car. I was told that the jury also came in for close attention from the boys. One woman juror was excused further service when she reported being threatened with a shotgun. Do I know who made the threats? What do you think?

We were only fighting fire with fire. It was common knowledge that certain police officers were going round to the houses of potential witnesses, nudging them to testify in a way that would suit the prosecution case. That was later confirmed in conversations we had with the Dunfermline boys. In fact, some witnesses even spoke about the police tactics while giving their evidence in open court. The Old Bill's strategy went something like this:

'Do you know Andy Blance?'

'I'm not sure,' the witness would say.

'Well you have to be sure. You don't want him getting away with what he did to your mate, now do you?'

When it came to jury selection the system also worked to my disadvantage. The trial was held in Dunfermline, where the 'victims' all came from. There was intense pressure on jurors to convict from their friends, neighbours and workmates. The trial should have taken place elsewhere, on neutral territory if you like, and not somewhere people could be got at. I was later told by a reliable source that a juror had been having a quiet drink when someone came into the pub and told him to 'jail the bastards'.

Despite the excellent work my mates had put in with the witnesses and the jury I knew that I was right up against it, as were the other three CCS in the dock. One of them, like me, had been charged with mobbing and rioting and attempted murder. We called him Mr Burberry, because he was always clad from head to toe in that brand of clothes. For a casual he came from a very unusual background. His father was a top civil servant, who had worked with government ministers, giving him the income to buy a house in one of the capital's most exclusive suburbs. Reflecting his dad's status Mr Burberry had been sent to a top private school, where he had passed an impressive number of O levels and Highers. He was certainly a flamboyant young man and in addition to the Burberry he insisted on letting his blond hair grow down to his shoulders. Inconspicuous he was not. The other two CCS were charged with the same offences as Burberry and me.

As I had feared from the moment I was arrested in Leith the scales of justice were heavily weighted against me. The prosecution relied to a large extent on identification evidence. Fair enough, but on the night in question I had been wearing a baseball cap (with, I always remember, the word 'Corfu' sewn into the rim) pulled right down to my eyebrows. To make myself even more anonymous I had tied a Newcastle United scarf tightly over my mouth and nose. All anyone could see was my eyes. The other CCS who were there that night had on similar disguises. How anyone could have made a positive identification, especially at that time of night, is beyond me.

When the Crown witnesses started to give their evidence these flaws became clear for all to see. One Dunfermline casual said he saw me that night without a covering on my face, which I have already explained was impossible. Another said I had been wearing a balaclava but he had been able to recognise me because he had seen my eyes, despite admitting his judgement was seriously impaired by the large quantities of drink and drugs – including acid – that he had ingested. In fact not one person who got up in that witness box gave an accurate account of what I was wearing. According to a university academic, who has made a study of the casual movement in Scotland, of the eight witnesses who said I had been there that night no less than six withdrew or significantly modified their statements.[7] The accounts given

---

[7] Richard Giulianotti, 'Keep it in the Family. The Social Ontology of Hibs Casuals' in R. and J. Williams, *Modernity and Identity in Global Football Culture*, 1993. This is one of several papers that Giulianotti, a sociologist from the University of Aberdeen, has written on the CCS.

by the other two, which I have discussed above, were hardly the most convincing. The same academic also notes that ten people who had been in the Kronk that night, and who knew me well, told the police I had not been there.

The boy I hit with the axe also gave evidence and testified that he didn't know who had struck him. That should have worked to my advantage. However, when he had finished giving evidence, which was on a Friday afternoon, he was arrested, kept in police custody until the Tuesday and charged with perjury. The Crown offered to drop the perjury charge if he went back into court and changed his story. After that, in my eyes at least, his evidence was all over the place and I think any fair-minded person would have had to conclude that his credibility had been shot to pieces. He wasn't the only one who wavered. In the dock several other Crown witnesses appeared to go back on their original story and they too were charged with perjury.

The level of witness intimidation was a running theme throughout the trial. The prosecution did its best to convince the jury that the only reason more witnesses weren't positively identifying us was because they had been threatened with violence by the CCS. If they could make that stick it would go a long way to securing a conviction. It was at that point they played what they thought was their trump card.

In the run up to the trial I had been arrested at a game against Celtic (on 9 March 1991) and taken to a police station, where I was searched. The cops found two pieces of paper with the names of Crown witnesses on them among my possessions, which, without my knowledge, they photocopied and put back with the rest of my stuff. That photocopied material eventually found its way to the Crown. It was important evidence and should have been disclosed to my lawyer as a production before the trial began. When I was called to the stand to give evidence the lawyer who was prosecuting pulled out the lists of names and asked if I remembered having them in my possession at the Celtic game. It was a bolt from the blue. I had forgotten about being lifted at the Celtic game and of course my lawyer knew nothing about the lists.

The impression they wanted to give was that I intended to intimidate the people on the list, another clear sign that I must be guilty. The prosecutor didn't get the chance to put a follow-up question. As soon as he asked me about the pieces of paper all four defence lawyers jumped to their feet as one.

'Objection!' they roared.

The trial was stopped and the court cleared to allow the judge to listen to legal arguments about the admissibility of the bits of paper. Although he agreed with the objection lodged by my legal team, and instructed the jury to ignore the pieces of paper, in my opinion the die was cast. It is like me saying to a friend that someone has been shagging his bird and then telling the bloke to forget what I had just said. He wouldn't, would he?

At the end of the trial I realised things did not look that great. The crucial identification evidence had gone against us, despite it being of the dodgy variety. In addition the jury would clearly have taken on board the allegations of witness intimidation. Then there were the infamous lists of names – despite being instructed to ignore them jurors are only human and I remain convinced they were a major factor in the decision that was reached.

As we waited for the verdict the atmosphere inside the courtroom was tense, as it had been from the start of the trial. The CCS had been out in force on the public benches from day one and the guys had given Crown witnesses and the jury the evil eye at every possible opportunity. The security was even more extensive than usual. It was probably necessary. The cops knew we could have sparked a riot. There were twelve CCS in court, with dozens outside, and the mood was ugly. For their part the Old Bill did their best to sweeten us up. Our families were allowed in to see us in the court cells, which was a real privilege and one not normally afforded to accused persons. A chief inspector came in to my cell and did his best to reason with me.

'I don't want any trouble up the stairs Andy, no matter how the verdict goes.'

'How can I do anything about that when I'm down here?' I asked.

'I know you've got ways and means to get word to them. And I know how influential you are,' he insisted.

'They are going to do what they want. There are fifty or sixty of them up there and there's nothing I can do.'

For better or worse this is how I am portrayed in the media.
(courtesy Mirrorpix)

Royal Nip, considered by many the spiritual home of the CCS.

The Albion, another favourite pub, and just yards from Easter Road.

The Hibs club store, one shop I don't shoplift from!

The so-called 'Bridge of Doom', where we attacked many away mobs leaving Easter Road; one unfortunate Motherwell casual even got thrown off.

We caused total mayhem on our trip to Liege in 1989.
I am pictured here, front left.

Anderlecht 1992. The Hibs players with the CCS flag after the game.
Contrary to what you read in the papers many players were fascinated with
the whole casuals' thing.

The CCS walking over the hill to Pittodrie in the 1980s.
Aberdeen was always one of our hardest away trips.

A recent CCS excursion to Bolton for a pre-season friendly
in the summer of 2009.

On the street

Walking through Glasgow in '93

A little scuffle with Aberdeen's mob, the ASC

On home turf: some of the boys marching through the Cowgate.

We took a huge mob down to Preston in 2005.

I am a dedicated Hibs fan, even following the team to the Ukraine in 2005. Bongo is on my right.

Mickey Weir, a Hibs legend, is pictured here wearing the club kit. (I am second from left.)

With Irvine Welsh at a pre-season game in Ireland in summer 2009. He is a true Hibby, a real party animal and of course a great novelist.

Kevin Thomson (left) now at Rangers and Scott Brown now at Celtic were both great players for Hibs. More importantly they are both great lads. This was in August 2009.

The appearance of a 'Magnificent Seven' of CCS on *Soccer AM* in
September 2000 provoked a flood of complaints from viewers
(I am on the far right). But it was nice to meet Helen Chamberlain,
a lovely down-to-earth person.

With my three sons, all proud Hibbys, outside Easter Road.
From left to right they are Kevin, Jack and Jamie.

'Oh come on Andy. We let your girlfriend and the other boys' families in to see you. You owe us.'

Perhaps because of my unwillingness to help they flooded the court with officers. We, the accused, had two cops alongside us, another one behind and a fourth in front of us. There were cops positioned next to the entrances and a big group of them outside the courtroom. All we needed now was the verdict and after five hours of weighing up the evidence the jurors streamed back to their seats.

Despite the questionable evidence the jury had been fed it was close: eight had voted guilty, six not guilty. Interestingly, Mr Burberry was found guilty by unanimous verdict, perhaps because his long blond hair was easily recognisable. One of the other boys pulled a not proven and walked free while the fourth accused had been let go due to insufficient evidence after the Crown evidence had been led.

I was right about the serious jail time. The judge, Lord Kirkwood, said that our behaviour 'could not be tolerated in a civilised society' and jailed me for five years for mobbing and rioting and attempted murder. Burberry got four years for the same offences. How did I feel? The *Dunfermline Press* reported that 'I showed little emotion and gave a thumbs-up signal as the sentence was announced.' The same couldn't be said for Burberry's family. As we were sentenced an anguished voice cried out: 'No, no. He's innocent.'

To be frank it was what I had been expecting. In fact I thought it could have been a lot worse than the five years, especially when you took my record into account. There had been no doubt in my mind that I would get found guilty and be given a lengthy sentence. With that in mind I had steeled myself for what the judge might do.

In terms of the conduct of the trial that too was what I had expected. I have never had that much faith in Scottish justice but that had put the tin fucking lid on it. I am not denying that I was there and I confess that I did hit the boy with the axe but the evidence against me was contradictory, misleading and in some cases just plain false. We did lodge an appeal and based it on two points: that the sudden production of the list of names by the prosecution had prejudiced the jury against me even if the judge told them to ignore it; and, secondly, that there had been intimidation of at least one juror. Needless to say it was thrown out.

My only consolation was that the CCS did go on the rampage after the trial was over and kicked seven bells out of any passing Dunfermline-ite who even remotely resembled a casual.

11
HEARTS: CHASING THE SCUM

My hatred for Hearts, the Scum, runs deep. I refuse to wear anything maroon or to get into a maroon car. I would never hire a car from Hertz. The only time I ever say the word is to warn my son about the 'Hearts' on the pavement; that is, the dog shit. And no one can say I haven't suffered for my passions: when I was a teenager I had the words 'Fuck the Hearts' tattooed inside my upper lip. When I told the tattooist what I wanted done he pissed himself laughing but went ahead and did it anyway. The pain was excruciating, but it was well worth it.

When it came to violence we didn't just take it out on their mob (of which more later) there was also their team. The CCS often came across Hearts players in the city. Many of them, especially those from Edinburgh, were somewhat anti-Hibs. The worst of the lot, in my eyes, is Gary Mackay, a dyed-in-the-wool Jambo who was born next door to Tynecastle and makes no secret of his disdain for my club. He makes great play in his autobiography about the special feeling he got from beating us. Well I would like to mention the special feeling we got from trashing his pub, which we seemed to do on a regular basis. Others I hate with a passion include Alan Preston and Paul Hartley; the latter, in my view, wound up the Hibs fans with his celebrations when he scored a hat trick in the Scottish Cup semi final of 2006.

There were confrontations with Scum players in pubs, clubs and restaurants. One night in the late Eighties six of us were in Buster Brown's – where, incidentally, we got treated like royalty – when we spotted Hearts midfielder Mike Galloway and two of his pals standing at the other end of the bar. We gave them the evil eye. And just in case they didn't get the message I whipped off my jumper, revealing a 'These Colours Don't Run' T-shirt imprinted with the Hibs Union Jack. Subtle it wasn't. Galloway and his mates now knew we were CCS and that violence was just a heartbeat away. He decided to try diplomacy and walked over to where we were standing.

'Look, we don't want any trouble,' he insisted.

I didn't give a fuck whether he wanted trouble or not. He was in 'our' club and we were the ones who would take the final decision on that, not him. Galloway had a reputation as a hard man on the field and I wanted to find out if he could handle himself off it. More than that, doing him would have been a real feather in our cap, something that would be talked about for years to come. In the end we decided that six of us against just three of them would have been a liberty and that is not the game we are in. He walked out of the club in one piece.

I still regard the Galloway incident as something of a lost opportunity. The plain fact of the matter is that I detest that lot. With Celtic and Rangers it is business. With the Scum it is personal. So you can imagine my feelings in June 1990 when Wallace Mercer, chairman of the aforementioned Scum, launched a takeover bid for Hibs. He claimed it was a merger and the aim was to create an Edinburgh superclub that would play in a brand-new stadium at Hermiston in the west of the city. The new club, Mercer argued, would be in a position to compete with the Old Firm, in fact with any club in Europe.

Of course, it wasn't a merger. It was a takeover. Mercer planned to shut Hibs, knock down Easter Road and redevelop the land. Hibs had massive financial problems at the time after a number of unwise, non-football investments by the board. In fact we were staring bankruptcy in the face. Mercer saw an opportunity and made his move.

I don't think I have ever hated anyone the way I hated Mercer. The Hearts chairman was a fat, Tory bastard from Glasgow whose first love was rugby and who knew very little, if anything, about football. I saw him for what he was: an arrogant, public-school-educated snob who spoke as if he had a corncob wedged up his arse. He didn't give a fuck about either Hearts or Hibs or the thousands of football fans in

Edinburgh who lived for their teams. He could never have appreciated just how deeply Hibs were rooted in the community and how strong our attachment to the club is. He was a money-grubber who had made his money in property and saw the chance to make a quick buck by putting starter homes for young executives on Easter Road.[8]

The prospect of Mercer's bid succeeding brought home to me how big a part Hibs played in my life. My house was, and still is, a shrine to the club, as is my body, which is covered in Hibs tattoos. I remember crying, aged just eight, when my favourite player Alan Gordon was transferred to Dundee. He is one in a long line who have been sold, usually down south or to the Old Firm. I cried too in 1979 when we lost the Scottish Cup final to Rangers after a second replay. Our last win in that august competition was in 1902, when we beat Celtic 1–0, and the hoodoo has continued into the twenty-first century. There have been good times, most notably the League Cup final win in 2007 against a Kilmarnock team stuffed with former players from the Scum. And victories in local derbies don't come any sweeter than the 6–2 pummelling of Hearts in 2002, when Mixu Paatelainen scored a wonderful hat-trick.

I also reflected on the club's glorious history. The Edinburgh derby is the second oldest in the world – only the Nottingham derby has been going for longer – and it has certainly been around for much longer than the Old Firm version. Then there is the Famous Five of Gordon Smith, Bobby Johnstone, Lawrie Reilly, Eddie Turnbull and Willie Ormond, who were, in the opinion of many knowledgeable commentators, the finest forward line in the history of Scottish football. They helped Hibs to win three league titles in the late 1940s and early 1950s and then made history in 1955 as the first British team to compete in Europe. In 1953 the Famous Five helped put English giants Tottenham Hotspur and Newcastle United to the sword (the latter by four goals to nil) as Hibs reached the final of the Coronation Cup.

[8] I am not the only one who felt strongly about the man. It was reported in March 2009 that Scotland's First Minister Alex Salmond (himself a Jambo) disliked Mercer, his politics, his attitude and his attempts to take over Hibs.

I thought about memorable European nights, like the time in 1960 when we knocked mighty Barcelona out of the Fairs Cup (a forerunner of today's Europa League) and reached the semi-final of that competition. And no Hibs fan will ever forget the result of results: the 7–0 demolition of Hearts on New Year's Day 1973, a result made possible by one of the best displays of attacking football ever seen in Scotland.

I was also proud of the club's local connections. Most of our fans come from Edinburgh and the Lothians, unlike Celtic and Rangers, who, because of their sectarian histories, draw support from all over Scotland and Ireland. I loved the fact that so many local boys have donned that famous green-and-white jersey, especially in the teams of the late 1980s and early 1990s. Guys like Mickey Weir, Keith Wright, Paul Kane and my favourite player of all time, Gordon Hunter.[9]

Thousands of Hibs fans felt the same way. A steering group called Hands Off Hibs was set up. There were marches and mass meetings, including a rally at Easter Road. A five-thousand-signature petition was handed into 10 Downing Street. Celebrity supporters, including the Proclaimers, joined in, while Hibby John Leslie even raised the issue on *Blue Peter*. There was support too from politicians, trade unions, the local council and the media. Even fans of the Scum opposed Mercer: an opinion poll in the *Edinburgh Evening News* showed a big majority of them were against the merger. Some turned up at our rallies.

While legitimate protest is all well and good we in the CCS quickly came to the conclusion that much stronger action was needed. Threats against Mercer were made through the media, in letters to Tynecastle and in anonymous phone calls. I am not saying we would have killed him but we had contingency plans to do him serious harm if the takeover looked like succeeding. I better just leave it at that.

As tensions mounted we visited his house in the exclusive Edinburgh suburb of Barnton. Our intention was to confront him, perhaps even to beat him up, anything to make him abandon the

---

[9] I admire Gordon mainly because he is a great Hibby – and not just because he broke Gary Mackay's jaw in the Edinburgh derby. Whether you meant it or not, more power to your elbow big man!

takeover. About twenty-five of us were there, including a number of scarfers. He wasn't at home that night so we had to content ourselves with painting slogans on his house. 'Mercer is dead', 'Long Live Hibs', that sort of thing. It wasn't long before the police arrived. They told us in no uncertain terms to leave and after that the house was guarded twenty-four/seven.

The campaign worked, especially, it seems, the threats of violence. Mercer abandoned his bid in September 1990, telling the *Sunday Mail*: 'My wife, son and daughter have been under constant pressure over the past six weeks – with threats, phone calls and so on. The police told me not to mention it because it increases the tension.' Wise man. If he had succeeded in putting Hibs out of business he would have needed the SAS to guard him for the rest of his life.

I never stopped hating Mercer and I never will. When he died, in January 2006, we celebrated. It was almost as good as winning a trophy. We made up a little ditty to commemorate his passing, which we sang to the tune of 'The Entertainer', the theme music from the hit movie *The Sting*.

Tell all the Hearts you know,
Wallace Mercer is dead and we're no'.
He's no longer here
So let's have a beer
Wallace Mercer is dead and we're no'.

Some good did come out of the Mercer saga. Businessman Tom Farmer (now Sir Tom) a native of Leith, decided to use some of his millions to prop up the club and to make us more businesslike. Now, in 2009, we are on a secure financial footing, and much better off, ironically, than that lot from across the city, who always seem to be teetering on the edge of bankruptcy.

Hibs will live forever and future generations will be able to recite my favourite poem:

HIBS BOY

In Leith the sun shines bright
High above a sea of green,
And on the field below
Is the greatest football team

✱

When it came to the Hearts casuals, hatred was not my primary emotion. It was contempt. Contempt for a mob that refused to engage with the CCS. Hearts were, and still are, a mob that skulks in the shadows. They are cowards, pure and simple. That is surprising because their predecessors from pre-casual days, the Gorgie Aggro, used to terrorise Hibs fans. The Aggro had a fearsome reputation, justifiably so. In the late Seventies, early Eighties Hibs fans would have to hide their scarves on the way to the Edinburgh derby, even if it was at Easter Road. The alternative was a beating. Of course that was true at almost every ground we went to. Before the CCS came along Hibs fans were fair game in Glasgow, Dundee and Aberdeen. Hell, I even remember us getting chased at rickety old Somerset Park, the home of Ayr United.

So the Capital Service Firm, the Scum's mob, had a lot to live up to. But they failed miserably. I am not entirely sure why that was but one reason must have been the attitude of the Hearts scarfers. They hated their own casuals; they just thought they shouldn't be part of football. In fact they often turned on the CSF and beat them up. It was a strange situation. So strange that in the years ahead some of the Hearts casuals joined the CCS. They were obviously so pissed off about being part of a shit mob that they were prepared to countenance anything, even if it meant joining the firm attached to their deadliest rivals.

My first run in with Hearts took place during the Edinburgh Festival Trophy in the summer of 1985. A combined Hibs–Scum team had been formed to take on Bayern Munich and the game was scheduled for Tynecastle. I was walking to the match with Robb and two girlfriends when we were surrounded by twenty CSF. I told Robb to run ahead and alert the rest of our boys, who were about three hundred yards away. As he ran to get reinforcements I started a heated argument with the CSF and then, when our boys arrived, I smacked the one nearest to me in the face. The guys then launched into the CSF, chasing them right back into Gorgie. They ran and hid.

After the game I was walking away from Tynecastle with Brad Welsh when we were surrounded by fifty CSF. I told Brad to go for help, leaving me alone with the cunts. They didn't waste any time, swarming round me like bees in a hive. I took a real beating and ended up with a burst nose and a swollen lip. It would have much worse if they hadn't been so closely packed, which meant that landing a clean punch or kick was that much harder. My ordeal didn't last for long. Our boys were soon on the scene and for the second time that afternoon we chased them. It set a pattern for the next twenty years or more. In later years we made up a little chant in their honour. 'Same old Hearts, always hiding.'

The biggest problem after that was finding their mob. When we went to Tynecastle they would be drinking in the Green Tree pub in the middle of Gorgie and as we went past they gave us dog's abuse, safe in the knowledge that the police would protect them. Unlike most other Scottish firms they would not front up like men. Sometimes we had to trade blows with the Old Bill to get at them; on other occasions we got lucky and were able to take them by surprise. One of those lucky occasions was in a busy Lothian Road pub. We got a phone call this night to say that the CSF were in a certain bar, having a right good time. It was an opportunity not to be missed and so we put together the biggest mob we could muster at short notice and made our way to Lothian Road. What a fucking fright they got when we burst in. The ones that did stand up and fight were quickly dealt with. At least they put up token resistance; the rest of them just bottled it. Their attempts to get away were frantic. Some of them locked themselves in toilet cubicles, others hid under tables, yet others scurried down the fire escape. It was a truly pathetic sight.

In almost a quarter of a century they only ever tried to come to our place twice and they certainly didn't manage to march down Easter Road on either occasion. On the first foray they got as far as the Mound, on Princes Street, but had to turn back when we came on the scene and laid into them. The second time was a little less farcical.

They reached London Road, less than half a mile from the stadium, before we pounced and gave them a kicking.

There were so many memorable victories and in so many different places: outside the Polwarth bar, in the Hopetoun pub, in front of John Robertson's pub in 2005, on Dundee Terrace in 2007. One of my sons even knocked out a CSF boy who just happens to be the son of a Hearts legend outside the Omni Centre. The only time they even came close to getting the better of us was when we were heavily outnumbered. There was one such occasion in 2005 when, after a Hearts versus Motherwell game, fifteen of us went hunting in Haymarket. There was no sign of the CSF but we got a call to say fifty of them were in the Standing Order pub in George Street. By the time we got there the pub had closed but we ran into them in Queensferry Street and there was a short, but extremely vicious, clash. Despite a three-to-one advantage in their favour it finished honours even.

The clash with the CSF that really sticks in my memory took place on Boxing Day 1992. I was then in Noranside open prison, a much cushier number than either Saughton or Glenochil. From time to time we were granted home leave and this was my first such leave in the course of my five-year sentence for the raid on the Kronk. We had been playing Falkirk but despite them having a tasty little mob, the Falkirk Fear, we had seen neither hide nor hair of them that day. Later, in the pub, fuelled by drink and disappointed by the absence of violence at the game, we had a mad idea: let's go and look for the CSF. So nine of us jumped into two cars and headed for Gorgie, where we parked outside a bingo hall. It wasn't our way to carry weapons but we made an exception on this occasion. After all we were likely to be heavily outnumbered by the Hearts mob and we had to even things up somehow.

We went into the car boots and fished out whatever we could find. Some boys wielded screwdrivers, while another had a wheel-brace; and I saw one armed with a hammer. I found a long, black, Maglite torch. We walked towards the Green Tree (later John Robertson's) pub. I was on the pavement about twelve yards in front of the others, who were on the road. One of their boys just happened to be looking out of the window and saw my eight CCS pals coming his way. He immediately raised the alarm and about thirty of them piled out.

As they walked towards us one of them, who knew about my prison sentence, recognised me. He shouted:

'Hey, Blancey, are you out for a holiday?'

Cheeky cunt.

'Aye, and I'm going to fucking enjoy it.'

I let the torch slide down my sleeve and into my hand. I lashed out, hitting one of them on the head with the Maglite. A foot-long metal torch makes a fearsome weapon and my blow knocked him off his feet and onto the pavement. No sooner had he fallen than my pals steamed in, slashing and hacking at Hearts with their car tools. As usual the CSF backed off and when we kept coming they panicked and scrambled back into the Green Tree. Some made it to safety but there was such an almighty rush to get back inside that many of them got caught in the doorway. Talk about shooting fish in a barrel. We didn't need an invitation and we waded in to the stragglers.

With the main job done we decided to round things off by smashing the pub's windows. Then, in the realisation that the cops would not be far away, we legged it. We hadn't got far before we realised there was a problem. In the confusion one of our boys had been left behind. Even though we could hear the police sirens in the distance we had to go back for him – leaving a mate behind just wasn't on. When we got back to the pub he was in a hell of a state. In fact he had been stabbed in the head with a screwdriver and was taking a real beating from the CSF. After pushing them back into the pub we took our injured comrade down a lane and to safety.

Our next problem was the Old Bill. By going back to the pub we had given up any chance of escaping their clutches. I was the first to be arrested, which could have had very serious consequences not only for my future home leave from prison but also for the proportion of my five-year sentence I would have to serve. Some quick thinking was called for. I started wheezing and gulping, pretending I was having an asthma attack. I asked the cop who arrested me if I could walk backwards and forwards to get my breathing going again. He agreed. But every time I went backwards I moved a little further away. Then, after four or five perambulations, I thought 'fuck it' and bolted.

Not having a clue about the best way to go I sprinted through a block of flats but ran straight into more Old Bill. They had just arrested two CSF, one of whom was the boy I had hit with the torch. His face was split open and bleeding. They were about to arrest me but I told them I hadn't been involved in the fighting and that I had already left my details with their colleagues. The cops seemed to believe me and were on the point of letting me go when the guy I had assaulted started shouting and swearing at me. The daft bastard was going to get me nicked so I told the bizzies the blow to his head had probably scrambled his brains. Taking what I said at face value one of them asked the other, non-injured CSF if I had been there:

'No. He wisnae there.'

'Are you sure?' asked the cop.

'Aye, I'm sure.'

That was good enough for the bizzies and one of them said:

'Right off you go. If we see you in this area again tonight you'll get arrested.'

'Of course, officer. I am doing my best to get out of here.'

I was grateful to that Scumbo. He could have put me in the frame for hitting his mate, causing me all sorts of problems with the courts and with Noranside. My home leave would certainly have been cancelled and I would most probably have been moved out of open prison and back into a mainstream nick. It was, if you like, the 'code of the casuals'. Never grass, not even on your bitterest rivals.

When I got back inside a funny story reached my ears. The boy I hit with the torch thought I had struck him with a frozen black pudding. I must have scrambled his brains after all.

It wasn't just confrontations between the two mobs that Hearts had to worry about. They got done all over the place: when they were out shopping, at work, in clubs, even at home and at their place of work. As I discuss elsewhere their boys often got 'taxed' in the city centre. In other words if they had been out shopping Hibs boys, mainly the Baby Crew, would mug them for their nice, new, designer clothes.

The CSF didn't fare much better on nights out. If they were alone or with mates in a pub or a club they got a kicking. If they were with a bird they were told to leave. And sharpish. It must have messed up their social lives no end! They had no comeback. In fact they couldn't even register a verbal complaint because any insult, real or imagined, was severely punished. Our boys would go to their house, or to where they worked, and teach them a lesson they would never forget.

No social life, no shopping, hiding before derbies, always looking over your shoulder for the next attack. It almost makes me feel sorry for them.

But let's not get carried away.

12
DOING TIME

I have spent a good part of my life in jails of one sort or another. The longest spell was after the Kronk, for which I got five years and served about three years seven months. Then there was the six-month sentence in Inverness and the four months in Perth prison in 1987 for fighting with the cop in Dundee. My other main spell behind bars was in my teens when I got sent to youth-detention centre. There have been a few other bits and bobs along the way for shoplifting and assault and breach of the peace, not forgetting the many police cells I have graced in Scotland, England and on the Continent.

Some people find it hard to come to terms with prison. I am not one of them. I coped well and my main challenge was overcoming the sheer boredom of life inside. When I stepped through those gates I made a conscious decision to get my head down, do my time and get out as quickly as possible. It helped that I didn't smoke or take drugs. That meant I needed nothing from my fellow cons and was therefore never beholden to them. It also meant the screws were more inclined to leave me alone.

The other thing that helped me was the support of family and friends. I got a constant stream of letters from CCS boys and from other pals. If someone was on holiday a postcard was sure to wing its way from foreign shores. I think I got an average of four letters a day, although my record for a single day was an incredible twenty-eight. The letters kept me up to date with Hibs, the CCS and what was happening in and around Edinburgh and Fife. The correspondence was a huge boost to my morale. Reading the letters, and then replying to them, definitely relieved the boredom and took your mind off things. But most of all you felt so grateful that people cared enough about you to write so often. It was the same with the phone. We couldn't make outgoing calls but I was inundated with friends calling me, so much so that I was nicknamed Busby, after the bird in a BT advert of the time.

The most important thing for any con is the visit and once again I got more than my fair share. The CCS came in their droves as did my pals from Fife. Nor, most important of all, did my family let me down. Margo brought Kevin, who was five when I first went inside for the Kronk, and Jamie, who was then four. Their visits were special but then you had to deal with the heartache when visiting time was over and they walked out of that door. As any con will tell you that is the hardest thing of all to bear.

As far as dad was concerned he would have come every week. As an honest and honourable man he must have been devastated by my part in the Kronk but that wasn't going to stop him visiting me. I have let him down so often but once again he stood by me. It was much more than I deserved. I tried to restrict his visits to once every three months or so. It wasn't that I didn't want to see him. I did. But I felt that he didn't deserve to be put through that ordeal every week. It must be hellish visiting a son in prison, especially when he has transgressed against everything you believe in.

*

Although I only served a couple of months in Perth prison it turned out to be the most dangerous period I ever spent inside. Perth isn't Scotland's most notorious or hard-line jail and so I wasn't expecting anything untoward when I was sent there by Dundee sheriff court in mid 1987, and certainly not what happened.

It all started quite routinely. I was allocated a six-foot-by-six-foot cell, which I was to share with two other prisoners. One was a Scouser, the other from Perth. The Perth boy stuck up a big St Johnstone flag on the cell wall. I didn't mind that too much so I made no comment.

If it had been a Scum flag it would have been ripped down without a by your leave and shoved where the sun doesn't shine.

There was a flurry of excitement early on. Scotland had played England at Hampden and dozens of English hooligans had been arrested, so many in fact that a contingent got sent up to Perth. English thugs in a Scottish nick. What do you think is likely to happen? As tensions mounted sideways glances led to verbal insults and verbal insults to fisticuffs. Soon a full-scale battle had kicked off. Although the screws eventually managed to put the lid back on it came too late for one English boy. He had been wearing a big sovereign ring and when he wouldn't hand it over one of the Scottish lads cut his finger off.

That fight was a mere detail compared to what was to come. One day, about halfway through my sentence, when I was getting on with my job in the kitchen, the riot bell sounded. We were told to go back to our cells sharpish. As I trudged along the corridors in a big pair of wellies I couldn't believe my eyes. There was smoke and dust everywhere and half the ceiling was lying on the ground floor of the jail. Then, out of nowhere, screws wearing helmets and brandishing shields – known in the nick as the Mufti Mob – appeared. They ushered me and another con into the doctor's waiting room.

I didn't know it at the time but the great Perth prison riot had started.

In the waiting room we began to piece together what was going on. There was loud shouting outside, which we realised was coming from cons up on the roof. They had ripped out pipes and dislodged slates, and were using them as missiles. And in an even more dangerous move they had set fires all over the prison. The whole place was in turmoil.

The doctor's waiting room was not a good place to be. By ripping out a bench and climbing up to a window we could see that the jail was being systematically torn apart. There were fires everywhere and to make matters worse the jail was starting to flood. There we were, locked in a room and in danger of drowning, suffocating or being burned to death. We had to get out and quick.

The bench came in handy again. We picked it up and used it as a tool to hack away the plaster round the door lock, a gruelling process that seemed to take forever and left us dirty and sweaty. Then, after half an hour of hard graft, we were free. But as we emerged into the corridor the Mufti Mob grabbed us and unceremoniously marched us to the chapel, where about fifty of our fellow cons had gathered. All that hard work and we weren't going to see what was going on in the riot.

To be honest, safe from what was going on outside, it made a nice change from prison routine. We played cards for a time and then the chaplain came in and gave us a nice little sermon, the gist of which was 'behave yourselves'. To help pacify us the screws handed out Mars bars, crisps and juice. Then one con jumped up on the stage, grabbed the microphone from the chaplain and began belting out 'Anarchy in the UK' by the Sex Pistols. A right good choice, given what was happening elsewhere. We spent that night in the kitchens, where I slept on a bag of potatoes.

The next day, with our hall in pieces, we were assigned to cells in another part of the prison.

*

I suppose my time in Perth helped prepare me for the five year-sentence I got for the Kronk in 1991, although it was obviously of a quite different magnitude. After being sentenced at Dunfermline High Court I was taken to Saughton prison in Edinburgh and put into what we called a 'dog box' to get processed. This was also their chance to check if you are a potential suicide candidate or if there is anything bothering you. I told them I was fine and I think they knew that with my form I would be able to handle things.

Next on the list was getting kitted out with prison-issue clothes and bed linen. The con in charge of dishing out the gear had been in the CCS and when he saw me he asked cheerily: 'How's it going Andy?' He made sure the gear he gave me was brand new, which was a real privilege, one not normally extended to new prisoners unless they paid for it with cigarettes or other goods. And, honour of honours, I got a top blanket. That may sound trivial but not everyone did. Even better it was a green blanket. My CCS connections were working.

When I got to D hall (used to hold prisoners before they go to another jail) it was recreation time. Everyone had been following the case in the papers, which meant I was a minor celebrity. I could feel them scrutinising me, weighing me up, wondering how I would fit into the jail's hierarchy. I was assigned to a cell on the upper landing, where prisoners the authorities think can handle prison are put. I noted that Mr Burberry, the other CCS boy convicted after the Kronk, was sent to a cell on the ground floor. The screws were not at all confident that he could handle life inside. After four weeks I was moved to Glenochil in central Scotland, where I served the bulk of my sentence.

There were some right hard bastards in Glenochil at that time, guys like Tam Bagan, a well-known Glasgow gangster. They were at the top of the food chain, what you might call the A-list celebrities, while we casuals were strictly C-listers. I found that the really hard men never threw their weight about. They didn't have to; one look from these guys was enough. Although I tried to keep my head down I did get into a couple of fights, although neither of them was planned.

The first came about when I was just being friendly. I went up behind a guy called Big Feg (he was from Ferguslie Park, a notorious housing estate in Paisley) and jabbed him playfully in the sides. Feg got the shock of his life and probably without thinking he swivelled round and caught me with a right uppercut. I have never been hit so hard and for a few seconds I thought my jaw had been broken. Feg was genuinely sorry for what he had done and apologised profusely. I accepted his apology. You don't take on a guy like that unless it is absolutely necessary.

My other spot of bother came when I was working in the kitchens at Noranside open prison, after transferring there from Glenochil. A weegie wanted an extra pie and came into the kitchen and asked me for it. I couldn't oblige him. There was a screw standing right next to me and I would have been in trouble. So he went back to his table, cursing me under his breath. A few minutes later the weegie reappeared in the kitchen, this time wielding a fearsome-looking knife.

'I am going to fucking do you,' he spat.

I was shiting myself. He had lost face after being refused the pie and in jail people in that frame of mind are easily the most dangerous. I couldn't afford to let him see how I really felt – showing weakness inside is never a good idea – but at the same time I had to try and reason with him:

'If you are going to do it, then do it. But I wasn't trying to insult you. There was a screw next to me and I would have been in trouble,' I explained.

'Aye well, okay then. But do that again and I will have you,' he growled, waving the knife a few inches from my face.

And with that he went back to finish his lunch. It had been the closest of close shaves.

Apart from those two little problems the worst thing about prison was the sheer tedium. I have probably never read as many books, written as many letters or done as many puzzles. It's not like today, where cons have their own televisions, computers, radios and even Play Stations for fuck's sake. In Glenochil there were fourteen cells around a corridor, with one television between us. So we could look forward to watching the telly once a fortnight.

I thanked my lucky stars I wasn't into drugs because the lengths some people went to for a fix never failed to amaze me. One guy on home leave inserted a syringe into his anus; another did the same with a tennis ball. Both were stuffed full of heroin. Drugs were smuggled in felt-tip pens, in trainers, through couples kissing at visiting time. The flow of drugs into prison can never be stopped, short of strip-searching every visitor. The main drug in my time was temgesic, tiny pills designed to ease back pain. If temgesic is ground down it can be snorted, giving the user the same sensation as speed. Heroin too was popular; one reason being that it goes out of the system quicker than a drug like cannabis.

*

In 1992 I was transferred to Noranside open prison after serving fourteen months (a third of my net sentence) in mainstream jails. It was a good number; it really is as cushy as people say. The strangest thing was visiting. Girls could wear the shortest skirts they liked and you could disappear with them for half an hour to the disabled toilet or even go behind a tree in the grounds. Nor were there the same restrictions on the numbers who could visit. I remember one time when the CCS were doing the security for a rave in Aberdeen and had hired a coach for the occasion. On the way north they stopped in at Noranside and told the screws they were there to visit Andy Blance. In fact there were so many CCS in the jail that the security status was changed to black, which, I believe, is the highest of all. It was the talk of the steamie for weeks to come.

Open prison was usually the first step towards getting parole and so it proved with me. In October 1993, after doing almost half of my five years for the Kronk, I got parole. I was of course only out on licence and any breach of the licence conditions would have seen it revoked and me back behind bars. So what did I do? What I should have done was keep my nose clean, but that is precisely what I did not do. In no time at all I was back into shoplifting with a vengeance.

There were three of us out this day on a thieving expedition to the Borders, but it went spectacularly wrong. The cops were quickly onto us and one of their patrol vehicles rammed my car. I was arrested and charged in Kelso and remanded back to Saughton. After two months inside I was sent up for trial and pleaded guilty to a reduced charge of reset. The judge had to take into account the time I had spent in jail so he fined me £250 and ordered forfeiture of my car, which meant I was free to leave the court. He didn't know I was out on licence but if he had it would have been revoked and I would have been back inside to finish my five years.

I was ecstatic. It was a real result. But my joy was short-lived. Two cops appeared at Margo's door that night.

'Andy's licence has been revoked. Tell him to hand himself into Saughton or to the nearest police station tomorrow,' one of them informed her, in a very smug tone of voice.

I just didn't want to go back inside, especially not to Saughton and so, when Margo told me about the visit from the bizzies, I made another fateful decision.

For the second time in my life I was going on the run.

I was a fugitive for about two months and during that time I tried to live as normal a life as possible, even going to Kos on holiday. Wild horses wouldn't have kept me away from the football, something that the Old Bill realised only too well. They almost got me before a game with Aberdeen but I got a tip off and hid in the roof space of the pub we were drinking in. They swarmed all over the boozer but did not think to check the roof. Another time, when I was out for a walk in Mussleburgh, two cops approached me.

'Have you got a minute?' one politely enquired.

'No problem officer.'

'Is your name Andy Blance?'

'Naw. Not me. You must be mistaken.'

'Have you got a tattoo on your forehead?'

Of course I did have a tattoo, but it was on my crown rather than my forehead. I was wearing a baseball cap and pulled the rim up to show them my forehead, but not far enough for the tattoo to be visible. They seemed happy with that.

With a 'Sorry to bother you,' I was on my way.

But there was a CID man on the other side of the road and he must have told the two uniformed boys it was Andy Blance after all. They came after me but I knew what was afoot and had scarpered. By this time the area was awash with cops and the only place I could find to hide was inside a wheelie bin. It did the trick and I lived to fight another day.

The bizzies were determined to get me and my details, including the registration number of my car, were circulated to every force in Scotland. So when I was out shoplifting I had to rely on cadging a car from my pals. This day I was in Lanarkshire, driving a borrowed car, when I was stopped. It wasn't that the cops recognised me. It was because my mate had forgotten to tax his car. I gave the cops his name and when he got the summons through the post I reimbursed him the money for the fine.

There was another close call in Leith, this time at a routine road-block at one in the morning. I was on home turf, as were the cops, so I was sure they would recognise me. I thought, 'I got away with it in Lanarkshire but I'm fucked today.' I tried my best to fool them, even pulling down the sun visor so that my face would be partly obscured when they walked towards me. It wasn't the brightest idea I've ever had: at that time of night it should have been a dead giveaway. A cop came up to the window, asked me a few routine questions, smelt my breath for drink and checked that the car was roadworthy.

'That's fine sir. Sorry for any inconvenience.'

I was rapidly going through my nine lives.

My friends and family were also watched closely. In fact they busted my wife's house, and my girlfriend's. The net was closing.

I had been living in Rossie Place in Edinburgh and had just moved to a new place in Morningside. The cops went to my old house, kicked in the door and turned the place upside down. I knew they would be at the new house before much longer so, after speaking to my then girlfriend, we decided to go up north and spend a few days together before the inevitable happened.

We ended up in Inverness, where, inevitably, we went out on a shoplifting expedition. Perhaps due to the stress of being on the run I hadn't taken my normal precautions and we were quickly spotted by three security guards. I wasn't for giving up without a struggle and I wrestled with them for all I was worth, which enabled my girlfriend to get away from the shop before they could lock the doors.

'OK. It's cool. I give in,' I told them, after we had rolled around on the floor for several minutes.

They let go. I don't know what possessed me. It may have been the pressure I was under. I took a running jump at the big shop window and tried to crash through the glass. It must have been pretty tough glass because I just bounced off and landed head first in the mannequins.

That was the end of my jaunt to the Highlands. The cops arrived, put handcuffs on my legs and arms and dragged me off to Inverness police station. After an initial court appearance I was remanded for three weeks until my trial. I got six months for the shoplifting and was also sent back to Saughton to finish my sentence. The only consolation was that the two sentences ran concurrently.

13
RANGERS: IN THE BELLY OF THE BEAST

Ibrox. Even the word sends a shiver down your spine. We were going on our most dangerous awayday and didn't we know it. Despite the banter and the bravado on the train there was always a large knot in our stomachs as we pulled into Queen Street station. There was excitement, anticipation, even an eagerness to get into the fray, but that was always mixed with a healthy dose of fear. The younger ones were the worst affected. They had heard all the stories from the older boys and now they were going to experience a game at Rangers for the first time. We did our best to reassure them. 'It'll be okay. Don't worry. Just listen to us and you'll be fine.' I am sure it went in one ear and out of the other. When you are scared nothing seems to help.

It wasn't that the Rangers mob, the Inter City Firm, was the best. It wasn't, not by a long chalk. In fact I never felt it could match us in any department. On a level playing field we would have battered them every time.

There were, however, two factors that made a trip to Govan so testing. The first was that so many of their boys went out tooled up, not only with knives but also with coshes, CS gas, ammonia, hammers, knuckledusters; anything that would inflict maximum harm on opponents. The other thing that made it such a difficult outing was the attitude of their scarfers. Unlike ordinary fans at other clubs a high proportion of the Rangers support would fight toe to toe alongside

HIBS BOY

their casuals. They would really get stuck in. I think their sectarian attitudes had a lot to do with it. A lot of Rangers fans saw Hibs as a mini Celtic. To those people we were Fenian bastards, even though no one in the CCS could give a flying fuck about religion. I am typical. I am not a Catholic, nor is anyone in my family. The only time I have ever set foot in a church is for a funeral or a wedding. I know that Hibs were Scotland's first Catholic club – formed in 1875 by a Catholic priest, Father Edward Hannan – but those days are long gone.[10] Nowadays, it is simply not an issue for the CCS or even for the vast majority of Hibs fans.

It is true that the CCS flag is a green-black-and-white version of the Union Jack but we only designed it that way to wind up the Old Firm. For very different reasons both Celtic and Rangers fans hated green being part of this symbol of Britishness. The Rangers crowd was particularly incensed by our flag. When we unfurled it at Ibrox the whole ground seemed to bellow as one: 'What the fucking hell is that?' and would then launch into the full repertoire of Loyalist and anti-Catholic songs and chants, from 'The Sash' to 'No Surrender to the IRA'. We often played up to their image of us by responding with 'Dirty Orange Bastards'. But these clowns didn't realise we were just taking the piss and by this stage in the proceedings the atmosphere in the ground was poisonous.

The contempt was by no means all one way. For our part there was no love lost when it came to Rangers. We hated the fact that so many of their casuals and scarfers were glory hunters. All over Scotland you see them getting on a bus every other Saturday to make their pilgrimage to Ibrox. Why can't they support their local team? Of course this has made Rangers (and Celtic) rich, enabling them to buy up promising young players from other Scottish clubs, most of whom are then planted in the reserves or on the bench. No wonder our football is so uncompetitive. And, at best, many Rangers fans seem to be very reluctant

---

[10] I am proud to note however that Hibs were pioneers of football hooliganism. In 1875 the Hearts captain, Tom Purdie, got chased all over the pitch by Hibs fans. I believe it was the first recorded incidence of football violence anywhere in Britain.

Scots. They have always loved Ulster but in recent years their affection for England has become very noticeable. Why the fuck would any Scot want to sing 'Swing Low, Sweet Chariot' a song strongly associated with the England football and rugby teams?

And don't get me started on how we were treated during the game. The police and stewards went out of their way to give us the maximum amount of grief. Cattle would have been shown more respect. We were rounded up, surrounded by bizzies, escorted everywhere and watched constantly by closed-circuit television. If we had the audacity to sing or chant the cops were on our case straight away while, all around Ibrox, the bluenose legions belted out their anthems of hate without a care in the world.

In Scottish football there is, of course, one law for the Old Firm and another law for everyone else. Nor did the CCS, or ordinary Hibs fans for that matter, get much protection inside the stadium. We were allocated seats in the lower section of the Broomloan Road stand, below the massed ranks of Rangers supporters in the upper tier. Throughout the ninety minutes we would be subjected to a hail of missiles from above: pies, plastic bottles, coins, hot Bovril, you name it. Even worse, their fans would piss into plastic cups and tip the contents of their bladders onto our heads. As a non-drinker I was particularly nauseated by the scent of beer-flavoured urine.

Given this background it is little wonder that our clashes with Rangers were so vicious. I was arrested three times in a row at Ibrox for fighting with the ICF, and received at least one heavy fine for my troubles. It was a rare occasion if nothing happened. One time, in the mid 1980s, I was on a platform at Buchanan Street underground station with three of our boys when we were set upon by fifteen ICF. I hit one of our attackers with a bin and punched another, who lost his balance and almost fell onto the railway line. Sensing an opportunity I jumped on top of him and shouted to his mates, 'You Rangers boys either fuck off or he's going under a train.'

They fucked off.

In the same station, about two years later, we were going up the escalator when the ICF surprised us, hurling bottles, bricks and even shopping trolleys in our direction. It all kicked off and the fight spilled out of the station and onto George Square. It was exactly the same at Easter Road. I remember one time in the mid Eighties when Rangers got tickets for our end and we chased them onto the pitch, forcing the referee to stop the game.[11] Around the same time, after a match, there was a particularly vicious fight with the ICF and their scarfers in Lothian Road. One of their boys got hit on the head by a paving slab while he was lying on the ground and suffered very serious injuries that needed hospital treatment. That incident was treated as attempted murder by the police and there was an appeal in the media for witnesses.

However, the most memorable encounter with Rangers came in 1987. In terms of the numbers involved it was perhaps the biggest fight of that era, at least in Scotland. It became known as the Battle of Paisley Road West. We had travelled by train, our favoured mode of transport, and got off at Queen Street. We were well mobbed up, with a firm of at least 150 that included all of our main boys. The CCS was at its peak at this time. We were by some distance Scotland's top mob and our swagger as we walked from the station to Glasgow's south side must have been clear for all to see. We loved to walk. It gave us a strong sense of togetherness, a feeling that we were a part of something bigger than ourselves, that we had a common purpose, that we were part of a family. Most of all that we were Hibs boys.

Rangers had spotters at Queen Street. As they phoned their pals with a report on our numbers I knew they would have been impressed by our cockiness and self-confidence. They must have realised it would take something special to see us off, something above and beyond the Saturday-afternoon norm. We set off with a definite spring in our step and after walking for about half an hour we reached Govan and marched along Paisley Road West. The tension was incredible and I could feel that something big was about to go off. Sure enough, as we passed a well-known Rangers pub the ICF stormed out, backed up by dozens of their scarfers. Most were carrying either bottles or pint

---

[11] The *Daily Record* printed an excellent photo of this incident, under the headline 'Chaos Reigns at Easter Road'.

mugs and soon the air was thick with flying glass. We ducked or used our arms to protect our faces and then, once they were empty handed, we charged. Without a supply of missiles they weren't quite so bold and we were soon chasing them down the street, dishing out beatings to any stragglers we managed to catch.

The skirmishes continued all the way to the stadium as the ICF regrouped and attacked us from front and rear, supported at every turn by their scarfers. We always had to fight at Ibrox but we reached new heights that day out of sheer necessity. I reckon there were upwards of eight hundred ranged against us at different times on that afternoon. If we had not raised our game in the way that we did we would have been going home in an ambulance.

Bar the usual verbal abuse nothing happened during the game, but we weren't about to let sleeping dogs lie. The pre-match entertainment on the way to the ground had whetted our appetite. We were hungry for more. When we left Ibrox we headed straight for the District bar, a diehard Rangers pub and a known haunt of the ICF. There was no way of knowing if they were in there but we thought it well worth the gamble. Without further ado a dustbin was thrown through the window followed by a volley of bricks and stones. With all the windows shattered we backed off. If they were inside it would give them a chance to come out and face us. There was a collective roar from the pub and we knew we were in luck. Their whole crew was inside and within seconds they poured out, backed up once again by their scarfers. I could see in their eyes that they were well up for it. We had taken a liberty, one of many that day, and to their way of thinking that should never happen to the mighty Rangers on their own patch.

As usual they were armed to the teeth. Some were carrying knives, others hammers, bricks or bottles, while one guy was even brandishing a car aerial. This was going to be some party. As the two mobs steamed in one of their boys aimed a bottle at my head. Instinctively, I ducked and it flew past, smashing loudly on the pavement. We were now on a level playing field and I caught him with a solid punch, kicked him in the balls and moved onto my next opponent. In the melee I landed a lot of good blows but I was also taking a few as the two firms merged into one. At the same time their numbers were being swelled by new recruits from the thousands of Rangers fans who were streaming away from Ibrox. We were now badly outnumbered and to make matters worse we had to face volleys of bricks and chunks of paving slabs. And, Glasgow being Glasgow, the ICF and their pals were well armed, which resulted in several of our guys either being stabbed or slashed.

Nevertheless, thanks in large part to our sense of togetherness, after fifteen minutes of literally fighting for our lives we were still holding our own. It was superb, inspiring even. We were in the belly of the beast and we were not giving an inch. I suppose eventually we would have succumbed to the sheer weight of numbers, but we were never to find out. The coppers had managed to force their way through the thousands of bluenoses who were trying to get at us. They drew their batons and went to work on Rangers, lashing out at anything that moved.

Although the bizzies arrested seventy-seven of our mob and many Rangers boys as well, I was not among them. I was part of a group of about twenty-five CCS that walked back to the city centre, all the while surrounded by thousands of angry Rangers fans. Exhausted by our efforts outside Ibrox, and with so many of our top boys in custody, we would have been slaughtered if it had kicked off again. But despite many threats from the massed ranks of bluenoses who shadowed us all the way to Queen Street we managed to reach the station untouched and boarded a train for Edinburgh.

Rangers were also our opponents when I was involved in the most bizarre occurrence in my entire career as a casual – when I had to take my lawyer to a game! It took place in October 1993 when Hibs and Rangers reached the League Cup final, which, as Hampden was being redeveloped, was to be played at Celtic Park. I had been released from Noranside prison on parole after serving three years four months for the Kronk. In the week leading up to the game I was contacted by the *Daily Record*, which was following up on a story it had been running about the CCS booking buses for the final. The journalist's angle was, of course, that the boys were intent on causing mayhem in Glasgow and he asked if he could write a piece about me as the original story had created a lot of interest among readers. I planned to go the game but was determined to keep out of trouble, not least because I was taking my two sons aged seven and six with me. There was also the small matter of my parole conditions; if there was so much as a whiff of trouble I would be back inside serving the remaining eighteen months of my sentence.

However, I made the cardinal error of trusting a reporter. When his story came out (on 20 October 1993) it was splashed on the front page of the *Daily Record* under the headline 'Casual Battle Buses Shock'. I felt that I had been well and truly stitched up. The article made out that I was intent on causing trouble at the game and I knew it had made me a prime target for the police. If I so much as dropped a sweetie paper I was likely to be arrested. So I phoned my solicitor and explained what had happened. We agreed that the only way to get around the problem was if he came with me. I also had to convince the parole board that the article was a misrepresentation of what I had said. So I went to the match with my two boys and my lawyer was there in case the cops tried to pin one on me. Everything went smoothly: the police left me alone and the parole board later accepted my version of events. The only problem was the game itself, which Rangers won 2–1. At least there was one happy member of our little group. My lawyer is a real bluenose and although he tried to hide it I know he was delighted that Rangers lifted the cup.

If honours were even after the battle of Paisley Road West that certainly wasn't the case in October 1994, when Rangers came onto our patch. I had been recalled to jail for the Kronk but the boys told me all about it later. They had been in touch with the ICF throughout the week, trying to arrange a meet away from the prying eyes of the police. By the mid-Nineties the authorities had become much more effective at controlling hooliganism, both inside and outside stadiums, and were well aware of the strokes casuals pulled to avoid detection. For that reason many fights were arranged miles away from the ground as it was the only way to prevent being rudely interrupted by the cops. The boys knew the express train from Glasgow to Edinburgh would be watched like a hawk so they told the ICF to catch the slow train, the one that stops at all the obscure stations. Get off at Slateford they told them, it is a quiet little station in the south Edinburgh suburbs, the last place the bizzies would expect a meet. The ICF agreed.

As usual the CCS did its homework and carried out a recce of the station and the surrounding area. To the boys' delight it was perfect for an ambush, with a large patch of bushes right across from the station entrance. About eighty CCS travelled to Slateford in a convoy of cars and taxis. Spirits were high; this was one outing they were determined to enjoy. When the boys arrived they hid in bushes or in shop doorways and waited for Rangers.

When the ICF emerged from Slateford station the boys were struck by two things. First there were only about fifty of them and they had been expecting a much bigger mob. While, secondly, many of them were lads in their teens while most of our group, by comparison, were in their mid to late twenties, battle-hardened thugs who had fought the best Britain had to offer. Being Glaswegians they were carrying a fearsome array of weapons: CS gas, ammonia, coshes, baseball bats and of course knives but despite this many of their younger lads looked nervous. Then, as Rangers edged tentatively onto Slateford Road the boys charged; some of them from behind the bushes, others from doorways and assorted vantage points. It was a classic pincer movement. The ICF were not only surrounded by Scotland's most formidable firm but they were also seriously outnumbered. They knew the game was up and when they heard that familiar chant of 'CCS, CCS' many of them went to pieces. Some even threw their weapons at their opponents and, by this time in a blind panic, they ran.

The boys gratefully picked up the discarded weapons and gave chase. Most of those they caught were in a state of shock, they were just too scared to offer any resistance. Put simply, they beat them to a pulp. There were Rangers bodies everywhere: in shop doorways, under cars, in the middle of the street. Some of them were bleeding so profusely that women came out of their houses and covered them up with blankets. A local woman saw a CCS lad kicking one of the ICF and shouted:

'Leave him alone. He's had enough.'

'No fucking way. If we were lying on the ground at Ibrox they would stab us.'

And with that he kept on kicking the poor cunt.

It took the Old Bill fifteen minutes to arrive, which is an age in a mob fight, and by the time our lot heard the wail of the sirens the job was done and they trooped back to their cars.

Fair play to Rangers. They did try to exact revenge for Slateford and they pitched up in Edinburgh with impressive numbers on at least two occasions. The first time they went to the Royal Nip on Easter Road, our favourite pub, but we had been banned by the management so they had a fruitless afternoon. Then, a year later, they finally got their own back on the CCS outside the rear entrance to Waverley station. It might have only been twenty-a-side but it was one of the most brutal encounters I can remember. They gave us a good hiding that day and I wasn't the only one who was glad to see the police arrive.

It wasn't just in Scotland we ran into Rangers. In March 1998 Hibs had yet again been knocked out of the Scottish Cup in an early round and had arranged a game against South Shields, an English non-league side. Ever the dedicated Hibby I borrowed my sister's people carrier and took five of the lads down to Geordieland. After being stopped for speeding outside Newcastle we arrived in South Shields, parked the car and walked a short distance to the quaint little stadium. It was a friendly against a non-league side, a chance for a nice day out watching Hibs without the pressures that a competitive match brings. Trouble was the last thing on our minds.

But when we got to the ground our scarfers were in a state of near panic. They told us there were loads of Rangers fans in the crowd and that they had been spitting on the Hibs fans and giving them verbal abuse. And of course they had been belting out the usual repertoire of anti-Catholic and Loyalist songs. Many of the Rangers fans were Scots who had settled in the north-east of England; others were native Scots who had travelled down especially for the game. But they had one thing in common – a desire to intimidate the 'Catholic' followers of Hibernian Football Club. I was enraged. It was a fucking liberty. We couldn't even play a non-league team in England without being harassed by these bigoted cunts.

The stadium was, as I have said, on the quaint side. It had a bar, in front of which were a number of picnic tables and benches. There were about a dozen Rangers fans sitting at the tables, enjoying a few beers. So, with my five mates in tow, I strode up to the nearest table and knocked their pint glasses for six.

'Do you want to sing your bigoted fucking songs now?' I asked.

The fuse was well and truly lit and a tasty little scrap ensued. We quickly got the upper hand and chased the Rangers boys right out of the ground and down a lane. They tried to make a stand but we were driven on by our anger at their behaviour and we leathered them. The police duly arrived but we explained that they had started it and were backed up by our scarfers and by locals, many of whom were disgusted by the sectarian chanting. The cops, for once, believed us and we were allowed back into the ground to watch the match. I didn't hear a cheep from the bluenoses after that.

There is no doubt that our clashes with Rangers were vicious. And you don't have to take my word for it. You can see it for yourself on YouTube. Our fight with them in Dundee on 25 January 2003 was captured for posterity by closed-circuit television and some clever boy added an excellent dance soundtrack and uploaded it to the site. It is a bit blurred but it gives some idea of what a real live ruck is like. The public seems to like it; there are a couple of versions on YouTube but the most popular one has already been viewed by more than 220,000 people. I am sure they enjoyed watching the CCS and Rangers going at it good style.

The down side of the YouTube video was that I was lifted five months later. The cops studied the footage and arrested me during a dawn raid on my house. I wasn't the only one, as twelve more of our boys plus five ICF and one Dundee Utility also got nicked. Along with the others I was charged with mobbing and rioting, pleaded not guilty and was bailed to appear at a later date. One of my bail conditions was that I got banned from every SPL ground in Scotland. Another one was that I had to stay in the house on a Saturday afternoon between noon and six in the evening. While the other boys who were charged were allowed to sign on at the police station and then go to the pub I was, as usual, singled out for special treatment.

But I can't really complain as I got a result at my trial, and walked from court as a free man. The mobbing-and-rioting charge was dropped and I then rejected an offer from the Crown to plead guilty to a lesser count of breach of the peace, after I reasoned that the police would not be able to make any charge against me stick. Thankfully, I was right.

14
EDINBURGH DAYS, EDINBURGH NIGHTS

I was never a part-time casual. I lived the life 24/7. It was my identity. It was who I was. So a fight once a week on a Saturday afternoon was never going to satisfy me. I needed something to fill the void, something that would give me my adrenaline fix. And I could always find that something on the streets of Edinburgh. In fact, my first appearance before the High Court had nothing to do with a fight at the football. It was all down to my need for a kebab at the end of a good night out.

The year was 1987. It was pre-season, late July early August. The Scum were due to play Everton at Swinecastle on a Sunday afternoon. On the Saturday night before the game I had been out in Fife with my brother and a few of the boys before driving into Edinburgh to go to one of our favourite nightclubs, Dillinger's, in Lothian Road. Someone came in at around midnight and said that Everton's mob were just down the street. We couldn't resist and we piled out of the club and hunted high and low for the Scousers.

It was a bum steer. Everton had either departed the scene or had never been there in the first place. As the disappointment set in so did the hunger pangs and about ten of us headed for a takeaway. When we got to the establishment in question, which was run by Turks, we immediately recognised one of the customers: it was a well-known Hibs player, who just happened to be drunk out of his tiny mind. He was waiting for a pizza but was angered when a Turkish guy behind him in the queue got served first. His professional training instantly kicked in: he started to shout and swear at the shop manager as if he was a referee who had denied him a penalty.

His protest fell on deaf ears. So one of our boys, trying to be helpful, snatched the pizza from the startled Turk and handed it to the Hibs player. That went down like a lead balloon with the Turk, who punched our pal full in the face. Seconds later some of the guys who were working in the shop jumped over the counter, brandishing their kitchen knives and kebab skewers. It was one of the most dangerous situations I have ever been in, and that is saying something. These cunts were in a total frenzy, threatening anyone in their path. If we were going to walk away in one piece we were going to have to come up with a strategy to defend ourselves, and quick. They say that necessity is the mother of invention and it certainly was that night. I kicked in the shop window and picked up a jagged piece of glass, as did several other CCS. As the Turks came at us shrieking like banshees I arced the shard of glass like a dart. My aim would have done Phil 'the Power' Taylor proud. It hit one of the Turks on the side of his head, splitting it wide open. His pals saw what happened and realising that we would fight fire with fire they backed off.

It was lucky no one got killed that night. We managed to come out of it without serious damage but one innocent customer, who was not part of our group, wasn't so lucky. He got slashed by a Turk and had his back opened right up. We learnt later that he was taken to intensive care in Edinburgh Royal Infirmary.

But that wasn't the end of our troubles. Someone had called 999 and a group of us were arrested out on Lothian Road. Six people were charged with a variety of offences, including assault and mobbing and rioting: four CCS, including me, another mate of mine and, astonishingly, the unfortunate customer who had been slashed by the Turk, even though he had done nothing wrong and had ended up in hospital fighting for his life.

At the trial in Edinburgh High Court confusion reigned. The Turks gave very specific and detailed accounts of what each CCS boy had done and what weapons we were carrying, even though, at least initially, we had not been carrying anything. The problem was that the detail varied from witness to witness. For us it was an open goal.

Under cross examination some of the defence lawyers, including mine, were easily able to discredit these witnesses and their convoluted stories. The result was I walked free after a not guilty. But one of my pals was not so lucky. The boy who had snatched the pizza and given it to the Hibs player got two-and-a-half years. That proved just what a great result I got. With my previous I would have been looking at a three stretch at the very least

*

In the summer of 1989 we got an unusual invitation. We were asked to protect marchers on the first James Connolly memorial walk, an event organised by Irish Republicans.[12] I remember exactly how it came about. We were in the Southside Snooker Club this day when one of the organisers came up to me.

'How do you fancy being stewards at the Connolly march?' he asked.

'But we're not Republicans and we're not interested in religion,' I protested, knowing that is how the vast majority of CCS feel about Irish politics.

'Some of the Rangers and Hearts casuals will try to attack the march,' he countered.

'Sold.'

This is not to say there would be no police in attendance. Due to the volatile nature of the Connolly march the Old Bill would be out in force but the organisers wanted us to provide extra protection. Our job was to surround the marchers, acting almost like a human shield, something that the bizzies would not do.

When fifty of us arrived that morning at King's Stables Road, which is just off Lothian Road, we could see this was going to be a hell

---

[12] James Connolly, the son of a manure carter, was born in Edinburgh in 1868. A trade unionist, socialist agitator and Irish Republican he took part in the Easter Rising of 1916 as commandant of the Dublin brigade. When the rising failed Connolly was executed by the British. The march, often the locus for serious outbreaks of violence, has become an annual event in the city.

of a day. There were already hundreds of Republicans there with their flutes, drums and flags, many of them wearing Celtic jerseys. They were surrounded by a large contingent of police. The marchers were happy to see us, and with good reason. Without us they would have been picked off by the bruisers who were bellowing sectarian abuse at them, police or no police. The Loyalists were no mugs. They were big, fearsome-looking cunts with shaved heads, Union Jack tattoos and Rangers strips stretched over their beer bellies. A few I recognised as ICF, others were older, perhaps in their late thirties, early forties and by the look of them they clearly had paramilitary connections.

Talk about the lion's den.

The cops were not best pleased to see us, especially since we were all wearing our favourite 'These Colours Don't Run' T-shirts. The way I saw it we were doing them a favour. The Loyalists were fucking raging that the march was going ahead and at some point they would have taken on the cops to get at the Republicans. We saved them a lot of aggravation.

The first skirmish was not long in coming. When the marchers reached the Grassmarket the Loyalists launched an attack. We started up the traditional chant of 'CCS, CCS' and steamed right back into them. It was a score draw. Somehow the bizzies managed to keep the peace until the end of the march, at which point it all kicked off again. The trouble started in the 'Pubic Triangle' (so called because of the number of pubs in the area with tits-and-ass shows) where we bumped into the boys from Hearts and Rangers. Later there were clashes in Lothian Road and the fighting culminated with a mass brawl in the Meadows.

Taking on the Loyalists was an unusual gig for the CCS. In the main they weren't casuals and they had nothing to do with football. But that was us all over. We weren't picky; we would take on all comers, anytime, anywhere. That was true of another mob we faced on the streets of Edinburgh, a mob with lots of muscle, a mob with lots of members, a mob that was always tooled up.

You've guessed it. The Old Bill.

I have had many fights with individual cops and I have taken my share of beatings in police cells. But, apart from in a football context, the CCS had never fought them mob to mob in a normal setting. That all changed after what became known as the Battle of Bristo Square in 1989. I was there that night but unfortunately I went home early and missed all the fun, although I was given chapter and verse by Dave Ritchie, who saw it all. This is what happened . . . .

The CCS had booked a pub in Leith Walk for a party to celebrate Girvan's release from jail and invites had been sent to every member of the mob we had an address or phone number for. The problem was that so many people were invited the bizzies got wind of it. With their usual spite they decided to spoil everyone's fun. When the revellers turned up at the pub they were told the party had been cancelled.

Not wanting the entire night to be ruined some of the boys headed for the Royal Nip, which is close to the Hibs stadium, while others headed for the Penny Black, another pub frequented by the CCS. Others went to their local or to bars in the city centre. After an hour or so the phone calls started. Go immediately to the Meadows pub on the south side of Edinburgh, they were told. The party was back on. The Meadows was rocking. There were more than a hundred CCS there, happily getting pissed and without any thought of trouble. But the bizzies just wouldn't let it go. They turned up by the vanload and shut the bar, forcing the boys to leave.

As they drifted off in groups of about twenty the boys were closely followed by Old Bill. One group was tailed at very close quarters by a couple of dozen cops, one of whom had a police dog on a leash. They were out to goad the boys, shouting to them that an early night would do them the world of good. This went on for a good few minutes, until the CCS contigent reached Bristo Square, which is close to Edinburgh University. By this time they had reached the end of their tether.

'Fuck it. If you want some come and fucking get it,' one of the CCS shouted, turning to face the cops.

And, to his astonishment, they did want some. The bizzies steamed in like a mob, punching and kicking the CCS, but making no attempt to arrest anyone. One boy got bitten by the police Alsatian; another was handcuffed to a wire-mesh fence and kicked about the body. There were skirmishes all over the street, with no quarter being asked on either side. Then police reinforcements arrived and the arrests did begin. Dozens of boys were lifted and taken to the police station on High Street. They were banged up five or six to a cell. It was a Friday night, which gave the bizzzies the right to hold them until the Monday morning. The scandal was that the Old Bill did not give them anything to eat and they had to rely on fish suppers handed into the jail by fellow CCS members.

In the sheriff court on the Monday morning it took several hours for a decision to be made on whether they were to be remanded or let out on bail. Eventually, the news came through. It was bail. The court, which was full of CCS and family members, erupted.

But that was just the beginning. It would be eighteen long months before all the trials were completed and during that time the boys who had been charged were followed everywhere by undercover officers. It was harassment pure and simple. But the filth got their comeuppance. The defence lawyers ripped the police witnesses to shreds, pointing out that if anything it should have been them in the dock for assault. The court accepted these arguments and the boys who had been charged either got a not guilty or a not proven. Quite right too, in my view. The police operation that night was not about preventing trouble. It was about intimidating the CCS. Clearly, the Old Bill thought we had got too big for our boots.

*

There were many fringe benefits that came from being a known face in the CCS. In those days it gave you a certain status in Edinburgh. You would expect to get treated better than ordinary punters in pubs and nightclubs but what none of us expected was how attractive our hard-man image made us to women. I was constantly surprised by just how much of a turn-on the CCS was to the fairer sex.

I am no oil painting. If you don't believe me just take a look at the photos on the cover of this book. But my looks were no handicap when it came to pulling women. Once they realised you were a leading casual, that was it. Moths to a flame. They were attracted of course – as women have been down the ages – by the hard-man image and by notoriety.

In the pubs and clubs they would come up and ask: 'Are you Andy

Blance?' They got a thrill from talking to Hibs boys. They liked to be seen with us, to be around us. Quite often boys would get into serious relationships with these women. Other times it was just a bag-off, as we like to call a one-night stand in Edinburgh. I have lost count of the number of women I fucked inside nightclubs or in cars outside. One that sticks in my mind took place in Buster Brown's, which was very much the club of choice for Hibs boys. A girl sauntered over and started talking to me. Her pals had told her I was Andy Blance, one of the top boys in the Capital City Service. She was clearly keen for me to have my wicked way with her and within minutes we were at it on the fire escape, my arse going like a fiddler's elbow.

However, my most unforgettable memories from those days relate to the women who were known collectively to us as the Blow Job Queens, or sometimes as the Gobbleinas. Their sole mission in life, it seemed to us, was to give the CCS boys as many blowjobs as they could handle. They popped up everywhere: in the pub, in clubs, on the train to away games. When we spotted them the excitement was uncontainable. 'The gobblers are here. The gobblers are here,' we would shout.

Why they did it I will never know. They didn't look or sound like slags and all three were quiet, polite and well-spoken. In fact it was even rumoured that one of the girls was the daughter of a senior Edinburgh policeman. We certainly weren't exploiting them and they weren't feeble minded or simple. They knew what they were doing and they enjoyed it, as we did. They had another interesting little personality quirk. They would never let you ride them. Oral sex was as far as they would go. Maybe they were worried about getting pregnant or catching a dose of the clap. Or maybe they just loved giving head.

The area around the Penny Black was the most popular spot for a gobble. The BJQs would take the boys up a shop doorway and do the business on them. They would finish one and move straight onto the next boy in the queue. It was a production line.

The girls appeared from nowhere. One Saturday afternoon, when we got off the train at Glasgow Central station, we saw the three of them sitting on a bench at the end of the platform. 'Come with us' we said and we walked together to Queen Street to catch the train to

Edinburgh. When we got on board there were, as usual, police watching us, one at either end of each carriage. But a minor detail like that didn't stop the Gobbleinas. They crouched down under those little tables and serviced every last one of us. The cops didn't have a clue about what was going on but they probably wondered why we were so quiet and contented all the way home.

With my frequent spells in prison I missed some memorable rucks and that also applied to the fun the CCS had with the BJQs. There was one afternoon in particular that is still talked about today and has become part of CCS folklore. I was told about it by Girvan, who, inevitably, was right at the centre of events. In the late 1980s Hibs were playing St Mirren away and the CCS had hired a coach to take them through to the game. Driving through Paisley the driver – who bore an uncanny resemblance to Starsky from the television series *Starsky and Hutch* – came to a low-level railway bridge. Unsure if the bus would clear the bridge Starsky asked the boys for advice. They knew it had no chance of making it but they shouted as one: 'Of course it'll go fucking under. Hurry the fuck up. We're going to miss kick-off.'

It doesn't take a genius to work out what happened next. Crash. The bus hit the bridge, badly mangling the roof. Well that's what you get when you ask the CCS a stupid question.

Somehow the bus managed to limp to the stadium where it dropped the boys off. During the game they ran into two of the BJQs and persuaded them to come back with them on the bus, which they did. According to Girvan their productivity was impressive. He reckons about forty boys got a blow job on the road back to Edinburgh. One CCS however was left out. He had decided to make his own arrangements. The boys saw him sitting there with his jacket over his lap. But the jacket was going up and down like a yo-yo. Girvan whipped the jacket off and shouted: 'What the fuck are you doing having a wank? You can get a fucking blowjob.' Needless to say he has never lived it down.

As I said the BJQs popped up all over the place. One night I was giving Girvan a lift to Fife from Edinburgh in a wee Escort van. We were driving along Buccleuch Street in Edinburgh when I spotted two of the girls:

'There's two of the BJQs,' I told Girvan.
'Get them in here,' he replied.
'No way. I'm not interested in a blowjob tonight.'
But he stuck to his guns. I don't think he was getting much at home at that point.
'Shout on them. Shout on them,' he insisted.
So I pulled in to the pavement.
'Where are you two going?'
'We're going to the Southside snooker centre,' I was told.
'But there's no Hibs boys there. Why don't you come with us?' I said, lying through my teeth.
'OK.'
One jumped in the back with Girvan the other sat next to me in the front. Within seconds I heard the sound of a zip being pulled down. Girvan was getting what he wanted. I turned to face my passenger.
Now it was my turn . . . .

★

It wasn't just women who liked being seen with us. A lot of Hibs players were fascinated by the CCS, especially in the early days when the violence was at its peak. Although they had to ritually condemn it in the media – no doubt after being leant on by the club – the truth was that they wanted to know all the gory details. In fact I am convinced that many of them, especially the boys from of the team of the mid-to-late Eighties, which had many guys from a real Hibs background, would have been in our ranks. I remember how keen the Hibs players were to get CCS gear. When we were playing Videoton of Hungary in the UEFA Cup during season 1989/90 we gave them all 'These Colours Don't Run' T-shirts. They were delighted. But we were one T-shirt short and a well-known player missed out. He was so keen to get his hands on one that he pestered Bongo for half the night.

I have always socialised with Hibs players, as have other members of the CCS. They are not embarrassed to be seen with me and they never criticise what I do. They no doubt reasoned that I was a helpful guy to have around. After all they were never going to get hassle from

Hearts fans, or casuals, in the pub if they were in my company. I had other uses: as a non-drinker I was often asked to drive them home in their very expensive sports cars when they got pissed, which I can assure you was a regular occurrence.

Some players had more destructive and expensive tastes. I am not just talking here about Hibs players; I have enjoyed nights out with players from a range of Scottish clubs. For these guys fame and fortune and the adulation of football fans isn't enough. I am talking here about cocaine. Why they got into it I will never know. It must have wreaked havoc with their bodies – they are after all professional athletes – but there was an even more dangerous side-effect. The people it brought them into contact with. Recently, I took a call from a well-known gangster. He was looking for the phone number of a guy who had fucked him about, probably over payment for drugs. That guy just happened to be a Scotland internationalist. For obvious reasons I can't name him, or even the clubs he has played for, but I hope he managed to make his peace with the gangster, who is not someone you would want to mess with.

Hibernian Football Club has of course always strongly condemned the CCS. You would expect nothing else. Yet very few of us have been banned from Easter Road and I, perhaps the most notorious hooligan of all, am a season-ticket holder and have been for years. You hear about Celtic and Rangers fans being banned all the time but Hibs don't seem to have gone down that road in a big way although a few younger guys have been banned in recent years. The only problem I had was in the late 1980s when I was on bail for attacking a policeman in Dundee; I got banned for a few weeks, but that was by the court, not Hibs.

I am obviously concerned that when this book comes out action might be taken against me. In fact I was so worried that I raised the issue with a senior club official:

'I've been approached to do a book. What would the attitude of Hibs be?'

'It depends on the content. If it brought the club into disrepute and encouraged hooliganism we might have to think about banning you,' he replied.

'What if I say hooliganism is wrong?'
'That would probably be OK.'

I was none the wiser after our little chat but I hope that Hibs don't ban me. After all I am one of the most faithful fans the club has, following the team home and away, on the Continent and at pre-season friendlies.

That ought to count for something.

15
CELTIC: THE DAY OF RECKONING

There is only one thing worse than having cups of piss thrown over you at Ibrox and that is being patronised by Celtic fans. Because both Hibs and Celtic play in green and white and were founded by Irish immigrants in the nineteenth century, it gives them an excuse to come out with all that Irish brotherhood shite. They have got it into their heads that we are their 'wee cousins' and they are always trying to claim us for Paddydom. They say things like: 'Surely you would rather Celtic won the Old Firm game' or 'wouldn't you prefer Celtic to win the league rather than those Orange bastards?' I think I can speak for all Hibs fans when I say that we don't give a fuck. Like Rangers they are nothing more than Weegies and I hate them all with a vengeance. Of course the problem is that most of them aren't even Weegies. They are glory hunters from Kirkcaldy, Inverness, Dumfries and Perth; people who should be supporting their local teams rather than getting on the bus to Parkhead every second Saturday.

Then there is that small minority of Celtic fans who sing the pro-IRA songs. To my mind they are the lowest of the low. Why do they revere an organisation that seeks to murder British soldiers, many of them, of course, Scots? Despite what Celtic fans might think no one now supports Hibs because they are Roman Catholic. Maybe in the dim and distant past some people did, but, believe me, that all died out years ago. I am a good example: I am neither a Catholic, nor am I from a Catholic background, and I went to a non-denominational

141

school. I couldn't care less about religion and it sickens me that the dinosaurs in the West of Scotland still harp on about it so much. Rangers want to be English or Ulster and Celtic want to be Irish. Why can't they be Scottish like the rest of us?

And despite what they say the Old Firm clubs have always played up the sectarian aspects of their rivalry. Why? Because it has made them rich. For them to come out with all that Bhoys Against Bigotry crap, and the bluenose equivalent, makes me sick.

As for their mob, the Celtic Soccer Crew, it was feeble. I never rated them; they never fronted up at Easter Road, preferring to hide amongst their scarfers until they reached the safety of the ground where they had a steel fence and the police to protect them as they mouthed off at us for the entire ninety minutes. Despite Celtic's vast support the CSC numbered only three hundred at its peak, a pathetically low number for a club of that size. The main problem for the CSC was their own scarfers; they hated the whole casuals' thing with a vengeance and turned on the CSC all the time. They often sang that little ditty:

It's magic you know
Celtic and casuals don't go

We could see how their scarfers felt about them any time we travelled through to Celtic Park; there was a good example of that in October 1987. On that day, as for most home games, they didn't dare go into either the Celtic end or the Jungle[13], simply because of the abuse they would have had to take. They had to make do with the main stand and that's where we headed too. We were immediately recognised by their mob and it all kicked off next to the pie stand when they threw hot Bovril over us. Unfortunately, the confrontation, such as it was, only lasted for a minute before the cops arrived and threw us out of the ground.

---

[13] The Jungle was a section of covered terracing directly across from the main stand at Celtic Park. The hardcore Celtic fans congregated there and belted out their pro-IRA songs. It was demolished when the ground was redeveloped.

But the most memorable ruck with the CSC in Glasgow took place the season before when we travelled through to the west for a league match. When we got off the train at Queen Street station the CSC were waiting for us in George Square. The cops immediately stepped in and sent the two mobs in different directions. I ended up in a group of twenty CCS and as we were marching to the ground we were attacked by fifteen Celtic. We quickly got the upper hand and chased them. But they weren't about to give up and soon came back for more; this time there were twenty-five in the group. But, once again, we sent them packing without too much difficulty. Celtic were getting shown up on home turf, a situation that no self-respecting mob can tolerate. We knew they would be back, no doubt in even greater numbers than before. And so it proved.

When the CSC attacked for the third time we were walking past the Barras, Glasgow's world-famous street market. There were now at least forty of them and they were hungry for revenge. And, this time, the cops were nowhere to be seen. A vicious fight broke out and because we were outnumbered two-to-one many of our boys were soon on the defensive. I could see real fear in their eyes and they expected a real doing or even worse. One of our guys was getting a particularly hard time; he was on the ground and being kicked and stamped on by three or four of their mob. I realised that drastic action was needed, so I picked up a sandwich board from outside a shop, ran up to the boys who were attacking my mate and smashed the board over the head of one of his assailants.

Both mobs heard the wood impacting on his skull, and, suddenly, the fighting stopped. For a brief moment everyone was rooted to the spot. Then they looked round and saw the Celtic boy out cold. It proved to be the turning point. The CSC realised that we would do whatever it took and I noticed their confidence visibly draining away. At the same time it re-energised our boys. We regrouped and set about Celtic with renewed vigour. They were soon on the run and we never saw them again that afternoon.

After all the beatings we had inflicted on them I am sure Celtic must have been desperate to get one over on us. And on a cold, crisp afternoon in November 1987 we discovered just how desperate. What they did that day was probably the most cowardly act ever perpetrated by casuals in Scotland. And what's more it could easily have led to many innocent people being killed.

It started off just like any other Celtic game at Easter Road: we looked for them on the way to the ground, but they were nowhere to be seen. That wasn't unusual; like the cowards they normally were they often hid themselves among their scarfers. But it did seem much quieter than usual, especially given the number of rucks we had had in the recent past. Then, when the game started, they were up to their usual tricks, mouthing off at us from behind a metal segregation fence. So far so normal, except that they seemed more confident and self-assured than they usually were on our patch.

With about twenty minutes of the second half gone we discovered just why they were so cocky. A Celtic boy hurled a metal object over the fence, which I recognised straightaway as a CS-gas canister. It was no doubt aimed at us but it flew right over our heads and landed in the middle of the main group of Hibs fans, who were in the covered terracing across from the main stand. Cue panic as the gas seeped out of the canister and was inhaled by everyone in the immediate vicinity. To make matters worse there was a strong breeze and it blew the gas right across the enclosure causing people to choke and cough. I will always remember the sound of women screaming hysterically and children crying for their mothers as the gas enveloped the terracing.

Before long there was blind panic as thousands of Hibs fans scrambled desperately to get onto the pitch and away from the gas.[14] The CCS had experience of being gassed by Celtic on a previous occasion so we stayed on the terracing in an act of defiance as much as anything else. We pulled our Burberry scarves over faces and shouted to each

---

[14] Lives could easily have been lost. The crowd that day was in excess of 23,000 and the Hibs enclosure was tightly packed with fans; many of them women, children and the elderly. In its report on the incident the *Daily Record* argued that there could have been a repeat of the Heysel-stadium tragedy of 1985 in which thirty-nine fans were crushed to death. The paper devoted its editorial to the incident, describing it as the 'work of morons'.

other not to rub it into the eyes. Then, as the gas cleared, we followed the scarfers onto the pitch, although our aim was to get into the Celtic end and sort out the CSC. The police immediately realised what we were about and started pounding us with their batons. Outnumbered, we were pushed back onto the terracing, frustrated that we couldn't get at Celtic.[15]

In all my time as a casual I have never seen my CCS mates so angry or so determined to exact revenge. The gas was a liberty, one that had to be put right without delay. Apart from anything else we were the top mob in Scotland and things like that could not be tolerated at Easter Road. Some of the boys left the stadium immediately and went to the Royal Nip to look for reinforcements. Come the end of the game there was going to be a reckoning with Celtic, police or no police.

As the crowd left the away enclosure we looked for their mob among the thousands of Celtic scarfers. They were easily recognisable simply because they were not wearing colours. We charged at the line of police who were trying to protect them and we were helped by the Hibs scarfers, who were also raging at the CSC. At the same time people were throwing bottles, cans and stones as anger mounted. A full-scale riot was on the cards. Many of the Celtic mob didn't want to come out and hung around the exits in the hope that the storm would pass. They were shiting themselves. It wasn't just the look of apprehension in their eyes. I could smell their fear.

We managed to break through the police lines a couple of times but the cops quickly regrouped and baton-charged us all the way down Albion Road. But if the CSC thought they were out of the woods they had another thing coming. We moved onto Easter Road and hid up shop doorways and closes. Then we struck, punching and kicking and stamping and gouging, showing them no mercy. I was in a shop doorway and battered a few unsuspecting Celtic boys as they walked past.

---

[15] In John O'Kane's book *Celtic Soccer Casuals* he claims that the CSC were also on the pitch at that time and it was them who pushed the CCS back onto the terracing. This is of course a complete fantasy; I don't ever remember them getting the better of us.

They had no chance and they knew it. Our adrenaline drove us on to even greater violence. I have never seen a mob as scared as Celtic were that day.

Despite having such a pathetic firm I have to admit that Celtic twice managed to inflict serious injuries on me. However, it is entirely typical of them that both came about after sneaky attacks. The first occasion was in 1986 before we played them at home. The two mobs were fighting at the junction of Bothwell Street and Easter Road when one of their boys ran up behind me and slashed the nape of my neck. At first I thought I had been punched or hit by a stone so I carried on fighting. But one of our boys saw what had happened and shouted, 'You've been fucking slashed.' I put my hand on my neck and found it was covered in blood. Sean Welsh pointed out the boy who had done it so I ran up and caught him with a volley of punches. He fell to the ground, still clutching his Stanley knife. At that point the bizzies appeared and lifted him for possession of an offensive weapon. They asked if I wanted him charged but I said no. My neck wound didn't need stitches but the attack left a scar and is a permanent reminder of Celtic's cowardice. My view has always been that knives should be left at home and that people should be man enough to rely on their fists and feet.

The second incident also took place in Edinburgh. It was November 1992 and I was out on weekend leave from Noranside open prison. After spending time in mainstream nicks at the start of my five-year term, I now had a much cushier number and had no wish to be sent back to a real jail like Saughton or to have my privileges at Noranside withdrawn. We were playing Celtic in a league match and I went along with the father and brother of a good friend. Neither had any interest in hooliganism and that suited me just fine as I was desperate to stay out of trouble.

But trouble has an uncanny knack of finding me. As we were walking away from Easter Road Celtic's mob spotted me and they wasted no time. About forty of them charged and such was the weight of numbers that they pinned me up against a wall. They were desperately trying to land blows and despite my desperate attempts at self-defence one boy hit me with a really sweet punch. I felt my front tooth move and I put my hand in my mouth and discovered it was no longer attached to my gums. In fact the punch had knocked the tooth right out and onto the ground. A few seconds later the police turned up and chased the Celtic boys. I found my tooth and went to hospital, where they managed to reinstate it to its rightful place in my mouth.

Although my tooth was sorted there was now another problem that had to be dealt with: I needed more treatment and would have to explain to the powers that be at Noranside how I came to lose the tooth in the first place. So I cooked up a cock-and-bull story about how my little boy had jumped on me when he was wearing a fireman's helmet and knocked it out. I didn't think for one moment it would be believed, simply because I knew what the governor was like. In my experience he was a stickler for discipline and the rule book and you will get some idea of his personality if you think of the screw played by Fulton Mackay in the comedy series *Porridge*. He also came across to me as an arrogant bastard; we called him God, simply because we were always told 'just call him God'. He never asked us not to call him that, which to my mind sums the man up. But I got a lucky break. He was away on holiday that week and one of the assistant governors dealt with my case. In *Porridge* terms this guy was more like Mr Barrowclough, a really gullible type. He accepted my explanation and I was able to go to the dentist and to keep my privileges.

There is another similarity between the two Old Firm clubs: what away fans have to put up with at the ground. Just like at Ibrox the police and stewards at Celtic Park seem to go out of their way to inconvenience us, while treating the home fans with kid gloves. I remember one game in 2006, when Ivan Sproule was sent off. Enraged by another refereeing decision in favour of the Old Firm some of our scarfers started breaking seats. My son Jamie, then aged nineteen, stood on his seat to see what was happening. All of a sudden three stewards grabbed him, clearly intending to throw him out. I shouted 'What the fuck are you doing?' They shat it and backed off immediately. Then, from the safety of the passageway, they gestured for me to come out. I refused but they came back with the cops and first Jamie was ejected and then Jack and I got the same treatment. That would never have happened to the Celtic fans, but we were treated like shit there, on and off the field.

So much for being their wee cousins.

16

A NICE LITTLE EARNER

I have never had what you might call a normal nine-to-five job. That is hardly surprising. With my record prospective employers weren't exactly queuing up to take me on.

'What do you like doing in your spare time, Andy?' they might have asked at an interview.

'Kicking fuck out of the Scum.'

'Don't call us . . .'

Nowadays I run my own business but in the dim and distant past, the Eighties and early Nineties, I relied either on muscle jobs – like nightclub doorman and shop security – or the dole for an income. Neither was very lucrative so I had to find a way of supplementing my earnings. That meant crime, and the only decision I had to make was which type to engage in. I have never been involved in drug dealing. I have seen too many people in both Fife and Edinburgh, many of them friends, ruin their lives by getting addicted to heroin or other Class A drugs. It is a seedy, nasty, hopeless world that devours everything in its path. Apart from that the sentences handed down for dealing tend to be on the long side and that I could also do without.

Nor did I have any desire to get into that other great cashflow business: housebreaking. I find the thought of breaking into people's houses distasteful. As the father of three children I have always taken the view that the home is sacrosanct. It is the centre of family life and should not be sullied by criminality. Even the Mafia rarely hits an enemy in the family home.

So I plumped for shoplifting and became part of a fairly sizeable gang made up of CCS boys and people I knew from both Edinburgh and Fife. In those days it was a relatively easy way to make a few bob. Two decades on it would be much more difficult, what with closed-circuit television and all-round better store security. Of course we occasionally got caught and had to do jail time. I was given short prison sentences for shoplifting by courts in Edinburgh, Inverness, Stirling and Dunfermline. My longest sentence, after being arrested in Inverness, was six months in Porterfield. Most of the time it was a fine. Like Fletch in the BBC comedy series *Porridge*, I accepted the convictions as an occupational hazard.

As I have already said my first shoplifting venture was at the tender age of four and it was a childhood habit I never grew out of. It got more serious when I moved to Edinburgh from Rosyth as a teenager. I needed to get my hands on the latest skinhead fashions. Later I wanted the labels favoured by casuals: Pringle, Trim Trab, Farah and the like. It was easy pickings and as time passed more and more of my mates got involved.

Our first goal was not to get caught. Getting banged up or being hit with a fine was bad for business. There is one type of shoplifter who doesn't give a fuck if he, or she, gets caught, who will take any risk imaginable. You've guessed it: the junkie. The need for a fix over-rides everything else in their pathetic little lives. By contrast, we took every precaution in the book and then some.

We were lucky to have such a large group of people we could depend on. Shoplifting is a team game and not something you should attempt on your own. Three was the best number for a group of shoplifters. A woman and two men. In the shop it meant that the female and one of the males could pass themselves off as a married couple, which made them appear normal and respectable, while the spare man acted as a spotter or decoy. If two men are out shopping together it tends to look more suspicious.

With experience we got slicker and more professional. When a new person came in he, or she, got detailed instructions not only on how to steal goods without being observed and on how to remove security tags but also on how to interact with colleagues and shop staff. Clothes too were important. We always dressed smartly. The men didn't put on a shirt and tie but they were always dressed in what you might call smart-casual. Sometimes they wore glasses, while the females would make sure they were fully made up. Outward appearances matter. If you look respectable people are more likely to give you the benefit of the doubt.

Timing was key. On a weekday shops were generally quiet and often there would only be one assistant to cover a large area of floor space. We waited until genuine customers were being served before making our move. Most of the time the staff were so busy that we were in and out without them even seeing us. If there was an assistant who wasn't serving it still wasn't an insurmountable problem. We knew the layout of almost every big shop in Scotland and would arrange it so that one of us manoeuvred her into the most advantageous position by asking about the goods on sale in that part of the shop. That gave the second guy and his 'wife' the opportunity to help themselves.

We developed our own little code. One of us would hold up, say, a jumper and ask: 'Do you like this?' If the 'wife's' answer was: 'Yes, that's quite nice. I like that,' it meant no one was watching and the 'husband' could nick it. If it was, 'No, I don't really like that colour,' it meant that an assistant was watching and so we put the jumper back on the shelf. We often stood back to back with an assistant yet were still able to stuff a garment down our trousers. If you've got the balls you can get away with anything.

We gave a lot of thought to what we stole. In general we targeted goods of the highest quality, the ones with the most profit potential. If we were in a clothes shop we would go for the most expensive designer jeans. Packaging was a factor. Jumpers – generally not wrapped up in cellophane – were among the best items to steal. We could easily get four from the one shop; two down the trousers and one under each arm, while our female accomplice would stuff two into her bag. Baby clothes were also a favourite, simply because they were relatively expensive and small enough to steal in large volumes. One of the few times I deviated from our tried-and-tested formula was when I lifted a life-size statue of Laurel and Hardy and walked out of the shop with it under my arm. Amazingly, I got away unchallenged.

I knew it was a crazy risk but, hey, what the hell, I love their movies and I just couldn't resist it.

It was a well-oiled machine. We would target a town, drive there early in the morning, park up and then hit the shopping centre. We moved from shop to shop stealing as much as we could in each one before moving on. It is amazing how many you can do in one day. Our average was between twenty-five and thirty. Once we had exhausted all the possible targets it was back to the car and then onto the next town or back home.

The car was an important factor in the equation. We always made sure that a decoy carried the keys and not the lead shoplifter or his female accomplice. If either of them got caught and the police found the keys it would have led to much more serious charges when they found a car full of goods. We would also have had our ill-gotten gains confiscated. For the same reason the 'husband' and 'wife' avoided speaking to the decoy in the shopping centre in case the cops put two and two together.

For the most part it worked well. We cleared out stores from Hawick in the Borders to Inverness in the Highlands, and all points in between. We found it was easier to steal things in small towns. The stores had fewer staff, poorer security and were generally the last to introduce new technology, such as closed-circuit television. Inevitably, there were some tricky situations. I remember one time in Falkirk when I stole a car vacuum. There were only two of us out that day but we had gone through our usual routine and were sure that the shop would not even notice that the vacuum had disappeared. The problem was that an assistant had just stocked the shelves and he realised immediately it had been stolen. To make matters worse he was one of those really conscientious twats who is always out to impress his boss. Just as we were leaving the shop he came out and said to me and my pal:

'Can you come back into the shop?'

'What for?'

'You know what for. You stole a car vac,' he replied.

'Here take the fucking thing,' I shouted, throwing the vac at him.

'You still have to come back to the shop. You stole it.'

With that he grabbed me by the arm and tried to shepherd me

inside. This was not in the script and I knew that something had to be done, and quickly, before his colleagues phoned the bizzies. So I got out of the arm lock and hit him with a neat uppercut, which knocked him onto his arse. I am sure his boss was duly impressed by his devotion to duty. We legged it and managed to get into the car and out of town without any further hindrance.

Another problem was that we often ran into boys from other mobs, especially those attached to the Old Firm, whose glory-hunting followers you find in every town in Scotland. These encounters, as you can imagine, often led to confrontation. One such incident occurred in St Andrews, the home of golf and the last place you would associate with football hooliganism. There were four of us shoplifting that day and our plan was to split our resources down the middle, with two in each team. But before we could get into our stride I was clocked by three Rangers, all members of the ICF.

I said to the others, 'Just ignore them. Let's do our work first and we'll take care of them later.' At that point a fourth glory hunter appeared. He was, it turned out, the ringleader and a real bigmouth. This guy clearly took it as a personal insult that a main player from the CCS and his mates had dared to come onto his patch.

'What the fuck are you cunts doing here?' he bawled. 'This is our town.'

We didn't want any trouble at that stage. We just wanted to get on with the job in hand. But this bastard wasn't about to let it go. He was practically foaming at the mouth. He would have to be dealt with.

I whacked him in the face.

The punch was so hard that two teeth flew right out of his mouth. It was a beautiful blow, one that Joe Calzaghe would have been proud of. But I wasn't unscathed. My hand was bleeding profusely and the knuckles had been burst open by the force of the blow. So deep was the split that I could see right through to the bone. The long-term consequence is that I now have no knuckles on my right hand.

The other Rangers boys were in no mood to continue the aggro after what had happened to their mate. They got him back to his feet and made tracks. I urgently needed to see to my hand so we went into a hotel toilet where I washed the blood and debris off with a paper towel. We couldn't have picked a worse place. The hotel was right next to the police station and as we were leaving we saw the Rangers boys going in, presumably to file a complaint. It was time to leave town and smartly. I admit my driving wasn't up to much that day but it is difficult to control a car when your hand is mangled and spewing blood.

Another expedition that involved violence took place on home turf, on Princes Street. I was out with one of my best pals from the CCS. He had his baby with him in a pram but was still able to help me by keeping an eye on the shop assistants and security staff. I had picked up a boxed video recorder from a shelf and was walking towards my mate. As I went past, without breaking my stride, I murmured:

'How does it look?'

'You're fine. Keep moving.'

I thought I was home and hosed but what I didn't realise was that I had been spotted by closed-circuit-television operators. They radioed their two colleagues on the shop floor, who followed me outside.

'Stop there!' a female guard shouted.

'That will be fucking right,' I thought.

Still carrying the video I sprinted down Rose Street Lane, chased by the woman guard and her male colleague. I had a head start on them and I reckon I would have got away with the video had it not been for the actions of a heroic member of the public, or, as I would call him, a fucking busybody. He was a delivery driver and his van was parked in the lane, blocking the pavement on one side and almost the whole road. He took up a position in the only place not blocked by the van, thinking he had me trapped.

Smart cunt.

I waited until I got right up close to Mr Busybody and whacked him over the head with the box, which, with the video recorder inside, made an excellent club. He fell in a heap to the ground with the box on top of him. Maybe in future he'll think twice about getting involved in other people's business.

Meanwhile, back in the shop, my pal had been lifted and after taking his details the cops quickly established he was a CCS member and that he had form. He denied having anything to do with it, so the cops showed him the footage from the closed-circuit system. One of them said:

'There you are. Anyone can see you are talking to him.'

'Was I fuck. I was talking to the bairn.'

Of course he wouldn't have dreamt of grassing me up. That's not what Hibs boys do. His stonewalling worked. The cops couldn't pin anything on him and I got clean away.

The only downside from that incident was my hairstyle. I had just got an expensive, Frank McAvennie-influenced blond perm, which made me very conspicuous. I went back to the barbers and got a number one – just in case.

*

Once we had a quantity of stolen goods we then had to turn them into cash and that needed a quite different set of skills. Marketing, selling, taking orders, arranging repayments. They are all in a day's work for the busy shoplifter.

We found that one of the most reliable ways to guarantee sales was to take orders from our customers. They ordered everything from us: power tools, baby clothes, electrical equipment, soft furnishings. It was like using the Argos catalogue. One of the most common orders we got was for ready-made curtains. A woman would go into a shop, look at the curtains, tiebacks and pelmets and make a note of the colour, fabric and size she wanted. We would do the rest. The result was she got her haberdashery at half price or even less. Another lucrative item from that time was the video recorder, which when it first came out could cost between £300 and £400. I reckon half the punters in the east of Scotland recorded their favourite programmes on machines we had stolen.

When we made the sale we didn't always get paid the full whack right away. Most of our punters weren't well off and relied either on benefits or on a very low wage. They wanted the stuff but they wanted it on tick. We knew that was the only way they could afford our gear so we were happy to oblige. We did our rounds every week, noting down their payments. It was quite expensive, doing all that running around. First we had to deliver the goods then we had to go back every week and collect the money. But we never charged them interest.

That would have made us loan sharks and we weren't about to inflict that on people who were often friends and neighbours.

Most of our customers paid on time. They knew what would happen if they didn't. In a few cases we had to use a bit of muscle. I remember one guy who repeatedly refused to stump up, despite threats to his health and wellbeing. We took him up to the Whins (a range of hills near Inverkeithing) and made him strip off. Despite his protestations we left the cunt there and dropped off his clothes at his house. He had to walk back home bollock naked. Needless to say he paid his debt in full later that day.

As time passed we found a much more effective way of turning our ill-gotten gains into cash. Refunds. Many shops at that time had a policy of giving you a cash refund on returned goods, no questions asked. Those that didn't – perhaps because they insisted on a receipt – would give you a voucher, which you could either spend on stuff you wanted or sell to a punter. We would nick up to twelve baby outfits from good old Woolies and take them back.[16] Because we didn't have a receipt we got vouchers in return. At £15 an outfit it was not to be sneezed at.

The refunds proved particularly useful for one of the boys. He needed a new kitchen but wasn't going to spend two or three grand on it. So he targeted a well-known DIY superstore that sold nice kitchens. He would steal, say, four doorbells at £60 a throw and when he took them back he asked for a cash refund, knowing of course it was the company's policy not to give one. They offered a voucher or goods in kind so he picked out a kitchen cupboard. Then the next week he would go to a different branch, do the same thing and pick out a gas hob or an extractor fan. It was like that Johnny Cash song, the one where he works in the Cadillac factory and steals the car one piece at a time.

We always tried to keep up with what was going on around us and that came in handy when we noticed how well a certain book was

---

[16] Woolies was by far the easiest store to steal from. Their security was abysmal. Perhaps that was another reason for them going bankrupt.

doing. It was Maggie Thatcher's autobiography, *The Downing Street Years*, which had just been published. Even at £25 a throw it was top of the best-seller's list and stacked high in every bookshop in the country. It was too good an opportunity to miss. We targeted a well-known Scottish bookshop and stationers, one that had branches all over the place. We would walk in and lift a couple of copies, then move on to another branch, where we asked for a refund. Perhaps surprisingly, every shop, without exception, gave us the cash. In fact when the refund was being processed one of us would be among the shelves stealing more copies. This pattern was repeated all over the east of Scotland. We made upwards of a grand on that book.

It's the only thing Thatcher ever did for us.

While the guys sometimes took the goods back we found it was far more effective to use women. Women are considered more honest than men and if they are well-dressed and have make-up on that makes them even more plausible. I don't remember any of our female accomplices ever being challenged by a shop. In fact one of the best operators was a girl that one of the mob had a relationship with for two years. They mixed business with pleasure and made a right few quid along the way. She became an expert, dressing and looking the part. She even learned to speak with a posh accent, simply because the mainly working-class shop assistant is less likely to question someone from a middle-class background.

The refund system came in handy when someone needed cash quickly. One time that girl and her boyfriend needed £450 to pay the rent. They had twenty-four hours to find it or face eviction. So they went out and stole a dozen pairs of jeans from a well-known gent's clothing chain. Then they went round every one of their stores in the Edinburgh area and asked for a refund. When the lad got knocked back from the first one he let his girlfriend go into the rest. The result? She got a refund for all twelve pairs. At £45 a pair that added up to £540. Enough to pay the rent, with a bit left over for a good night out.

After two years he split up with that girl, both in a business and personal sense. As in most relationships there had to be a division of the joint possessions. But they didn't fight over who had bought the CDs or the coffee mugs. Their argument was over the ownership of the store vouchers! Finally, he agreed to take the Woolies vouchers for the simple reason that he was setting up home elsewhere and could use the vouchers at sister company B & Q.

Making a bit of pocket money wasn't the only reason I got into shoplifting. To be honest I loved the buzz, the thrill you got from stealing from under the noses of big shops, their security staff and the police. While it may not have been in the same league as fighting with the CCS it came a close second. The people around me noticed the effect it had. I used to give myself the day off on a Friday, perhaps taking back a few items for refunds if I could be bothered. One Friday, when I had been crabbit to my girlfriend, she snapped:

'You know what your problem is? You haven't had your fix.'

'What are you on about,' I replied, mystified.

'You haven't been out fucking stealing. You're like a junkie who hasn't had his fix. That's why you're shaking.'

I laughed but I knew deep down she was right.

We didn't entirely restrict ourselves to shoplifting. In our teenage years we had another sideline: stealing motors. We would go to car parks in Edinburgh and Dundee, usually in the middle of the day, to look for good prospects. Then it was just a case of using an automatic centre punch to put the window in.[17] Once we were inside we hotwired or 'poled' the car.[18] We targeted sporty cars, motors that the driving enthusiast loved. We would then transfer the registration details from an accident-damaged car that was the same make and colour to ours and sell it on. Sometimes we stole cars to order, so that the cash was guaranteed before we went out. We normally got around £200 for a car that would cost the buyer £2,000 to £3,000 in a garage.

In general it was a piece of cake, especially if you were careful. We always made sure that we wore our seatbelts, kept our speed under the

---

[17] An automatic centre punch is a small, sharp tool. If it is pressed against a glass surface it will break the glass and then retract automatically. It broke car windows quietly and efficiently.

[18] 'Poling' means placing a scaffolding pole over the ignition barrel and giving it a sharp jerk. That would break the ignition barrel off and we then used a screwdriver to start the engine.

legal limit and that no one did anything daft like throwing litter out of the window. It invariably worked, but, as with shoplifting, the car game could get you into the occasional scrape. One time we stole a motor and were driving it away from the scene, happy that the job had gone without a hitch. However, we didn't realise that some nosy cunt had seen us and phoned the filth. The next thing we knew we were headed straight for a police roadblock.

One of my accomplices screamed, 'You can't stop. They'll recognise us.'

So I drove up slowly, dropping down the gears, giving the impression that I was going to stop. Then when we were just a few feet away I accelerated hard and burst through the plastic barrier. When we got a safe distance from the cops we dumped the car and made our way home on public transport.

I gave up shoplifting and nicking cars almost twenty years ago. It wasn't that the shops were becoming better at detecting us, or that I had lost the edge. It was for family reasons. By then I had two young children and I wanted to spend more time with them.

It was time to join the legitimate business world.

17
SCOTLAND'S OTHER MOBS

Football hooliganism in Scotland is not just about the big clubs. Some of the little guys also have excellent firms. What they lack in size is more than made up for by their strong sense of local pride and a determination to stick it to the big boys. They tend not to travel well, just like their teams on the park, but at home they can be formidable, just like their teams on the park. I have had my moments with the likes of Airdrie's Section B Boys, the Falkirk Fear and St Mirren's Love Street Division.

The firms attached to the little clubs were always highly motivated when they faced Hibs. After all we were the nation's number one and that is motivation enough for anyone. This occasionally led them to go over the top. For example, we were in Paisley when a nutter from the Love Street Division pulled out a knife and tried to stab me in the stomach. I shouted on one of our boys to help me and while he distracted the knife man with a feint I punched him and wrested the knife from his hand. But in all honesty, outside of Glasgow, Edinburgh and Aberdeen there were only two mobs worth talking about: the Dundee Utility and the Motherwell Saturday Service.

Dundee, the City of Discovery, has two football clubs: Dundee and Dundee United. Neither side is part of what you might call the Big Five of Scottish football, which most people would agree consists of Celtic, Rangers, Hibs, Hearts and Aberdeen. The city's hooligans must have realised at an early stage that they would never become an effective force if they fought under two banners; they just wouldn't have been able to turn out enough boys. So they did the sensible thing and joined forces, calling themselves the Dundee Utility. This sense of unity was no doubt helped by the fact that the two stadiums, Dens Park and Tannadice (United), are less than a hundred yards apart.

The Utility had a reputation as one of the better Scottish mobs. They were more like Aberdeen or us than Celtic or Rangers. That is because, in the normal course of events, they did not pull knives on you. We had many a tussle with the Utility but I can honestly say that they only came out on top on a few occasions. I wish I could say the same for the Dundee Old Bill.

We always fronted up in Dundee, right from the early days of the CCS. My earliest memory is of standing on the terracing at Tannadice, one Saturday in 1985. I had a Chinese throwing star in my pocket, which I hoped to use at some stage. The problem was that the police did a pretty good job of stopping us getting at the Dundee boys. With our frustration growing we turned to the line of cops separating us from the home mob. We pushed into them, landing punches and kicks wherever we could, trying to break through to the other side. It was no good. There was no way through and when police reinforcements arrived I was nicked and taken to Bell Street police station. Thrown into a cell I was brought before the court on the Monday morning where I pleaded guilty to charges of breach of the peace and carrying an offensive weapon and was fined £75.

If that day was a damp squib I can have no complaints about my next visit to the City of Discovery in December 1986. In fact it was one of the most memorable of my hooligan career. Hibs had been scheduled to play Dundee United and Dundee within the space of a week, both away from home. The first match was just before Christmas and about fifty of us went through. Nothing happened either before or during the game but as we left Tannadice and walked past some council allotments we ran straight into the Utility. I could see right away that we would be up against it. We were well outnumbered. They had about eighty boys and the advantage of home turf. Despite giving it our best shot, the CCS, for the only time in its history, came a cropper against them. In fact we got a fucking good hiding. We consoled ourselves with the thought that we would only have to wait a week to get our own back.

A few days after Christmas we were back in Dundee, this time with one of the biggest mobs we had ever put into the field. There must have been three hundred CCS in Dundee that afternoon, all desperate to avenge an unlikely defeat. The Utility took one look at the size of our mob, and the determination etched on our faces, and stayed well out of the way.

The Dundee police were also concerned about the numbers we had put on the streets. Their response was heavy handed and ill judged. The plan was to marshal us into an orderly line and then frog-march us all the way to the ground. The problem was that we didn't appreciate being treated like cattle and told them where to get off. After a bit of pushing and shoving the mood on both sides turned ugly and fists began to fly, at which point the bizzies drew their truncheons and started to batter us. We responded in kind, as we always did.

Within a matter of minutes we had them on the back foot. I ran at one of the boys in blue, fully expecting him to stand his ground and fight. But it seeemed to me he momentarily lost his nerve and got on his toes. I chased him down a side street and saw him duck into a courtyard. Wrong move. There was only one way in and one way out and I had him just where I wanted him. I caught him on the side of the head with a beautiful right hook and followed that up with two more punches, one with my left and the other with the right. He offered no resistance and slumped to the ground holding his face. Knowing that the whole area would quickly be flooded with police reinforcements I bolted. But there was no chance of escape: when I got out of the courtyard and back on the street it looked as if every cop on Tayside was on the scene. They regained control and lined us up outside an art gallery.

An impromptu identity parade began. The cop I had battered, who now had a bruised and bloodied face, walked up and down the line three times trying to find me. I hid behind one of our taller boys but on his fourth attempt he found me.

'Oh, it's you. Now I know why you were hiding.'

Along with six other CCS I was arrested and taken to the station, where the charges against me were police assault and breach of the peace. As I flopped onto the mattress in my cell I had a good idea what was coming next. I wasn't naive. I had hurt one of theirs and now they were going to hurt me. That was the way it worked in those days. Why else would they put me in a cell on my own when the others were sharing? I only had a few minutes to wait.

The cell door burst open and three cops, all with grimly determined looks on their faces, marched in. What followed ranks as the worst beating I have ever had. They must have kicked me more than a hundred times. And every time I squealed it seemed to encourage them to kick even harder. The cop from the courtyard wasn't there and, as he continued to put the boot in, one of his colleagues explained why.

'You know what this is for. It's for our guy who's lying in the hospital.'

I must have punched him harder than I thought.

The cops did their best to make the rest of my stay in the nick as uncomfortable as possible. I got no food that night and on the Sunday morning all I was given was a dry roll and a cup of cold tea. I asked for water but not a drop was forthcoming. This was a clear breach of the rules, as water is meant to be given to prisoners whenever they ask for it. If they were going to play games then so was I. There was a WC in the cell so I grabbed my mattress, stuffed it into the water and flushed the toilet, causing my cell to flood. That soon got their attention. A bizzie walked in and asked:

'What the fuck is a' this aboot?'

'I've had fuck all to eat since I came in here. I asked for a drink of water and they wouldn't give me that either. This is my way of protesting.'

After that their attitude changed. It wasn't that they gave a toss about me. They just didn't want the hassle. I was given a book to read. I also got my lunch, which they probably spat on. I did make a formal complaint about what had happened but it was dismissed out of hand. I should have known better. These guys always stick together.

Despite what happened to me I was still facing a trial, which took place in April 1987 at Dundee Sheriff Court. There were five CCS in the dock: a boy we called Gogs and I were charged with police assault and breach of the peace while the other three were charged only with breach of the peace. I pleaded not guilty to both charges, reasoning that no one had seen me punch the cop in the courtyard. But there was no chance I was going to get away with it. A policewoman went into the witness box and testified that she saw me assault her colleague. I certainly didn't see her and to this day I find it hard to believe that she was anywhere near the courtyard. Still, it was the corroboration the prosecution needed and things now looked less rosy. Then, during a recess, I got a break.

The Crown spoke to my lawyer and said that if any three of us pleaded guilty to breach of the peace the charges against the other two boys would be dropped. It seems the prosecution just wanted three bodies, and it wasn't that fussy about who they were. They probably thought that the evidence against Gogs and me for the alleged police assault was a bit dodgy and were therefore prepared to cut their losses. It was a real lifeline. Because of my record I knew that I would get jail time on either count. So all I had to do was to persuade three of my pals to plead guilty to breach of the peace. Unfortunately, they didn't want to play ball. I did my best to persuade them to hold their hands up for a breach. I pointed out that as none of them had previous convictions for anything serious they would walk out of the court with a fine. I even offered to pay their fines, but they refused point blank. So much for one for all and all for one.

I knew that I was now looking at some fairly serious jail time and my lawyer advised me to change my plea to guilty on both charges in the hope that the sheriff would look more favourably on me. Then the prosecution came up with a new deal. If Gogs and I held our hands up for the police assault the breach-of-the-peace charges against all five of us would be dropped. The three of them then quite brazenly tried to persuade Gogs and me to accept the offer, despite their earlier refusal to help us in similar circumstances. I was enraged and pointed out just how two-faced they were being:

'A couple of hours ago you had the chance to take the deal but you said no. Now you expect me to do it for you.'

A heated argument ensued. In fact we very nearly came to blows in the dock and had to be restrained by the cops. In the end I had to take the deal; at least the breach of the peace was being dropped and that was something. I got three months and a week later another sheriff added on a further three months for a shoplifting conviction. I was taken down and delivered to Perth prison to begin another spell inside.

Although they could be a tasty firm on home soil, the Utility never once gave us any sort of a challenge in Edinburgh. In fact they rarely came through in numbers. In 2000, they hired buses and about sixty of them made the journey. Unfortunately for them the Old Bill found out and sent the buses back to Dundee. Fair play to them, they hired taxis and landed up at West Port in Tollcross. We had been waiting for ages for them to show their faces and most of us had just given up and gone to the game. It meant that about twelve of our lads were left to face sixty Utility. Needless to say, in the initial skirmishes the Utility got the better of things and our lads made a tactical withdrawal. This gave them the chance to regroup and to pick off smaller groups of Utility, which they did very effectively.

But the Old Bill had the last word. They hired a bus, forced the Dundee boys to get on board and sent them back home.

*

If the Utility had a very small mob compared to those from Glasgow, Edinburgh and Aberdeen then the Motherwell crew, the Motherwell Saturday Service, was minuscule by comparison. To be fair to them Motherwell was one of the first in Scotland to adopt the casual fashions and lifestyle. Although, let's face it, if you live in a dump like Motherwell, which is in the heart of industrial Lanarkshire, there is probably not that much else to do. The SS might have been small in numbers but they made up for it in viciousness, something that I discovered to my cost. They were also strong at home and could give bigger firms a decent run for their money there.

There were certainly some tasty scraps in and around Fir Park. In 1987 we went through to Motherwell and headed straight for the pub. After a few beers we began walking to the stadium, looking all the while for the Saturday Service. We soon found them or should I say they soon found us. There is a cluster of football pitches close to Fir Park and as we were crossing them they came out of nowhere, attacking us from three sides. It was a classic ambush tactic. And they were well mobbed up. If we didn't do something, and quickly, they would have done us serious damage. We needed to find somewhere to stand our ground, somewhere they couldn't get in behind us. So we ran as fast as we could into a housing estate and lined up in front of a block of flats. Sure enough it evened things up and we battled away happily until the cops arrived and restored order.

As I said their boys could be vicious cunts, as I learnt to my cost on another mid-Eighties trip to darkest Lanarkshire. This day I had my hands full fending off two Motherwell when one of their mates sneaked up behind me and hit me hard on the head with a brick. He succeeded in slicing off a small part of my ear, which I can assure you is a very painful experience. I thought I would at least get some sympathy from my mates but there was no fucking chance. Derek Dykes had been standing close to where it happened and had seen it all. He was pissing himself.

'What the fuck are you laughing at? He's taken off a bit of my ear.'

'Sorry mate. It just looked so fucking funny.'

With friends like that . . .

Motherwell weren't good travellers. Any time they plucked up the courage to come onto our patch it was a disaster – for them. In fact one of the greatest coups in our history came on just such an occasion. It was 18 February 1989 and we had been drawn to play them in the Scottish Cup at Easter Road. It was an important cup tie and we knew they would want to front up and generally give a good account of themselves. We were right. In fact we found out that they were planning to send a huge mob, at least by their standards, through to Edinburgh. We knew this because one of our boys lived in Motherwell and had got wind of their plans. They were obviously pulling out all the stops to put one over on us, to give us a hiding that would be remembered for years to come. We decided to come up with something big of our own, something that would put the cheeky cunts back in their box with the lid firmly shut. And our plan, in my humble opinion, was the stuff of genius.

The strategy was simple: do unto others as they would do unto you. On the morning of the match we hired half a dozen mini vans and drove through to Motherwell. We got there about eleven and parked next to the Arnold Clark garage. Then we walked up the hill to Fir Park, where we saw the Saturday Service getting ready to board their bus. Without further ado we charged right into them, delivering volleys of kicks and punches. To say they were surprised would be an understatement. In fact they were well and truly gobsmacked. After the battering we gave them they never did make it to Easter Road that day.

When they did set foot in Edinburgh it was something they lived to regret. In December 1988 the SS ventured into the Dunbar end at Easter Road. Although it was the area reserved for away supporters we decided to go in there and wait for our chance to strike. It came when Hibs scored. We celebrated, they suddenly realised who we were and it kicked off big time. Although they put up a good show we were just too strong. Around this time we were at our peak and we certainly weren't going to let those clowns get the better of us.

Motherwell were in just as much danger outside the stadium. I vividly recall that after one mid-Eighties league game they were carefully shepherded out of the ground by the bizzies and pointed in the direction of the metal footbridge in Bothwell Street. Although the police blocked it off if Rangers, Celtic or the Scum were the visitors it was the traditional route for away fans from smaller clubs going back to their buses or to the railway station. We knew that if we were cute we could get in about them, so we waited until they were on the bridge and then we struck, charging right into the back of their column. Thanks to the element of surprise, and with the advantage of superior numbers, we quickly got on top and taught them a very important lesson: it doesn't pay to front up at Easter Road. When a mob is taking a beating it usually has the option of retreating. But that didn't apply here. The bridge is so narrow that they were falling over themselves as they tried to get away, making it even easier for us to put the boot in where it hurt. One of their boys was taking particularly heavy punishment; in fact he got a real kicking. He must have thought that things couldn't get any worse, but by Christ they did. Four CCS picked him up and started to swing him from side to side. Judging by his hysterical pleas for mercy he must have known he was going to get thrown off that bridge.

Thud.

I will never forget the sound that poor cunt made as he hit the ground. It is easily twenty feet above ground level. He was lucky not to be killed, and although I never found out what happened to him it would have been a miracle if he had escaped serious injury.

To be fair to Motherwell they have, like us, been instrumental in trying to keep organised hooliganism alive in Scotland. We are of course swimming against the tide of history. The Old Bill, with their intelligence units, closed-circuit television and banning orders, have pretty much got us in their pockets. The result is that compared to the glory days of the Eighties and Nineties fights now are rare and when they do go off they involve much smaller numbers. So it was refreshing in 2006 to find myself in a vicious little confrontation with Motherwell. In the week of the match, which was at Fir Park, the Hibs Baby Crew had been on the phone constantly to their counterparts in the Motherwell Baby Crew to set something up for the Saturday.

I went through to the game by train, which meant changing at Bellshill in Lanarkshire before making the second leg of our journey to Motherwell. Our group consisted of me, my 8-year old son, Bongo and his niece and several members of our Baby Crew. When we got to Bellshill we had to walk up the stairs and over the railway line to get to the platform for the Motherwell train. As we climbed the stairs I noticed five Motherwell on the platform opposite. I didn't want to spook our Baby Crew so I kept quiet. When we came down the stairs, one of the Motherwell boys landed a kick on one of our Baby Crew while another of their lads weighed in with his fists. Unfortunately, the other Baby Crew were rooted to the spot and stood and watched as their pal took some hefty kicks and punches. I realised the urgency of the situation, edged forward and chinned one of the Motherwell boys. I threatened the others with more of the same, which made them back off. It gave the Baby Crew time to get on the train, where Jack, Bongo and I joined them.

Some fucking Baby Crew! I tore strips off the little fuckers for standing by and watching while one of their friends was taking a beating. Where was their team spirit I asked? You always back your pals; that is the first rule every CCS member has to learn. Next time they would have to do better.

By the time we reached Motherwell our presence was well and truly expected. The Saturday Service would be out for revenge after what had happened in the railway station. Three of their boys 'joined' our group in the town centre and walked alongside us. One of them got on the phone, looking for back up. For once I acted as peacemaker. We had young kids with us, including my son, and I didn't think it would be right to kick off under those circumstances. So I asked the boy on the phone to leave it out. But he ignored me and made several more calls looking for reinforcements.

I knew that within ten minutes there would be twenty or more of them in attendance and that some of us, maybe even the kids, would get hurt. Drastic action was called for and so I punched the mobile-phone boy full in the face. He went flying and fell against a passing car. But his calls had been effective because, just seconds later, about ten of his pals turned up. This time the Baby Crew did react. We picked up plastic baskets from outside a florist, emptied the flowers and attacked Motherwell with the empty baskets. They were surprisingly effective in a tight spot. The Motherwell boys obviously agreed and they were soon on the run.

That was strike two. But we knew that three strikes would be beyond our capabilities. There were too few of us and too many of them. And, in addition, they would be desperate for revenge after being shown up on their home patch. We were safe until after the game but when we came out we could see dozens of them hanging about, looking for the chance to pounce at some point between the stadium and the railway station. We would have been taking our lives in our hands. So, discretion being the better part of valour, we jumped onto a Hibs supporters bus, which took us home without any further drama.

*

Dunfermline Football Club was the closest team to my childhood home in Rosyth and it is also the closest to my current home in Inverkeithing. For that reason I have always had a bit of a soft spot for the 'Pars'. I like to see them doing well, unless of course they are playing Hibs, and over the years I have been friendly with many of the Dunfermline players. But when it came to their gangs it was a different story. My first time in prison, of course, was the result of mobbing and rioting in the Abbeyview area of Dunfermline, while the CCS attack on the Kronk disco came about after I had been harassed by Dunfermline street gangs and casuals.

The two major battles between the CCS and Dunfermline's Carnegie Soccer Service[19] were both keenly contested. After all it was almost a local derby, with Dunfermline less than twelve miles from Edinburgh. Another factor was that during my time as a casual Hibs were always among the elite of Scottish football while Dunfermline bounced between the top division and the lower leagues. So when an opportunity came up the two mobs grasped it with both hands.

The first really memorable encounter with the CSS was prior to a Scottish Cup tie in 1987. They took the train to Edinburgh and got off at Meadowbank station, before walking along London Road to Easter Road. When they came into view I was impressed. There were more than 150 of them, the biggest Dunfermline gang I had ever seen. I was in a little group of five, with Girvan, Sean Welsh, Rab Grady and another boy whose name escapes me; an advance party if you like.

About fifty yards behind us there was the main body of the CCS, which numbered about a hundred. But we weren't about to wait for them. We ran straight into the middle of the CSS, kicking and punching for all we were worth. Just behind us were the rest of our boys, running at full pelt. Dunfermline must have been astonished when the five of us attacked. I can imagine what was going through their minds: if five of them can do this much damage what will it be like when the other hundred get here? They panicked, turned tail and ran for their lives.

We chased them into Bothwell Street and about forty of us managed to get among them before the bizzies blocked the road off. Although

---

[19] The CSS was named after Andrew Carnegie, who was born in Dunfermline in 1835. Carnegie emigrated to America with his family in 1848, later becoming the world's richest man. A noted philanthropist, who gave away $350 million during his lifetime, Carnegie established many public libraries, including one in Dunfermline.

the CSS now outnumbered us their bottle had gone and we hammered them. It was like shooting fish in a barrel. Only one of their guys (whom I would later work with on the doors) stood and fought. Girvan took good care of him, knocking him to the ground, and he ended up lying semi-conscious in a large puddle. At least he had had the guts to put up some resistance. The rest were cowards.

A year or so later, in 1988, we paid them a visit. Dunfermline had just been promoted to the premier league and we were keen to stamp our authority on them from day one. It was one of our bigger travelling mobs, about three hundred I would estimate. There was a good dust up with the CSS after the game, when so many got arrested that the cops had to double and treble up the cells. But that's not why I remember the day so well. Before the game about forty of us had crowded into the bar of the City Hotel. We were drinking the place dry and the atmosphere just got rowdier and rowdier. It didn't take a genius to work out that the pub was going to get trashed. Aware of a problem the doorman marched in and shouted:

'Fucking drink up and every fucking one of you get out now.'

It was a red rag to a bull. One of our boys picked up a pint glass and aimed it at the doorman's head. I remember him screaming in agony. The glass had taken his eye right out.

As far as I know the CSS only got the better of us once, and that was very much due to force of circumstances. It happened in early 1991, in the wake of our attack on the Kronk. A lot of us had been charged with that incident and were out on bail awaiting trial. Many boys, perhaps understandably, didn't want to get into any more trouble with an appearance in the High Court hanging over their heads. Others were reluctant to go back to Dunfermline for fear of being lifted for the Kronk, even though they had been nowhere near the place. Me? I didn't give a fuck. What else was I going to do? Sit at home and worry about a trial that might not even result in a guilty verdict? Or get out there and watch my beloved Hibs with the prospect of a fight thrown in for good measure? It was no contest.

Not many of my fellow CCS took the same view, which is why only about a dozen of us pitched up in Dunfermline that day. The CSS must have thought they were onto a good thing because when we left the station there were about sixty of them massed in High Street. They were carrying bottles and glasses from the pub they had been drinking in. One of our boys picked up a traffic cone but I shouted to him:

'Put it down. We won't need it. Their mob is shite.'

I was right. They are shite. But it didn't save us that day. There were too many of them. Some of us got a real going over and I remember one boy being taken to hospital when his head was split open by a bottle. I put it down as a glorious defeat. We were outnumbered but we didn't run. We stood our ground and went down fighting.

You can't do any more than that.

18
ENGLAND'S FINEST

Being a Hibby is special. The family atmosphere, the strong sense of community; the strength you develop from experiencing so many disappointments and near things. I wouldn't change it for the world. If I had to mention a drawback it would be the lack of glamour games, the thrill that other fans must get from taking on the top teams at home and abroad. Celtic and Rangers get to the Champion's League and are drawn against Barcelona, Bayern Munich and AC Milan. On the rare occasions we get into Europe it is via the second-tier competition, which in the past was the UEFA Cup. We would come up against Videoton of Hungary or FC Liege – haud me back!

It was the same with pre-season friendlies. The Old Firm play Man Utd, Arsenal or Liverpool. Hibs get Preston, Bury, Walsall and Telford. It was as if the club bought that book *Crap Towns* and picked their friendly games from its pages. Having got that off my chest I suppose it did give us a chance to test ourselves against English opposition. And to be fair most of the mobs we came up against could fight.

My first experience of English mobs in their own backyards was in the summer of 1988. Hibs had arranged a mini-tour of the Midlands and the North that took in games against Walsall, Bury and Oldham. We didn't see any action at Walsall. There were only a few carloads of CCS there and all we came up against inside the ground was a few Rangers fans waving, guess what, Union Jacks. It was obviously meant to wind us up but the only thing we exchanged that afternoon was insults.

The next leg of the tour was no better because as far as hooliganism was concerned Bury were a washout. They didn't have a mob.

Our last stop was at Oldham. The game was on a Saturday, 6 August, which meant that we could turn out a sizeable group. About two hundred CCS came down by car or rail, including me. I had gone home after Bury and came back down on the train. It turned out there wasn't a service to Oldham from Edinburgh so we got off the train in Manchester after drinking the bar dry.

Some of our boys were friendly with a few of the Oldham boys, and they agreed to help us find Man City's mob. So we met up with three of their boys in the city centre and without further ado went looking for City. After checking out a few pubs we got lucky. About twenty of them were drinking in a bar called the Brunswick Cellars, which, as its name indicates, is in a downstairs cellar. It was perfect. There was only one way in and no back door or side entrance. The other problem for them was that there were a lot more of us, probably around a hundred. They had no fucking chance. We wiped the floor with them, trashed the pub and left.

Our good mood after battering City didn't last long. Arriving in Oldham we found out that our Baby Crew had been battered by Oldham's main mob, despite putting up stern resistance. Oldham were cock-a-hoop about what they had done to the Baby Crew right from the moment the referee blew his whistle to start the game. They obviously thought they had done our main mob. The stupid cunts. We got there late but as we filtered into Boundary Park, our faces as dark as thunder, I think it began to dawn on Oldham that they had made a mistake. A very serious mistake.

The Old Bill knew we were raging and near to the end of the game they tried to lock the gates at the back of our section of terracing. Fuck that. If they succeeded we would never get a crack at Oldham. So we laid into the cops. The gates stayed open and we were able to exit the terracing at the end of the game.

It was then we discovered that the police were one step ahead. As we tried to leave the ground we came up against an immoveable object. More gates, this time big, heavy, wooden, exit gates, which the cops had locked. At around fourteen-foot high they would be impossible to climb. And if we climbed over the turnstiles it would only be in small groups, making it easy for Oldham to pick us off. It looked like we were stuck and that Oldham would get away with what they had done to the Baby Crew.

We might have left it like that if Oldham hadn't continued to taunt us. They were dancing like dervishes outside the ground, goading us about the beating our youngsters had taken. We snapped and just launched ourselves at those gates. At first it seemed like an impossible task. In fact it must have looked comical because Oldham were creasing up at our efforts to break through. But gradually, very gradually, we began to make headway. Our anger spurred us on and with more than a hundred bodies running at the gates something had to give. And then, suddenly, we were through and steaming into our tormentors.

Fuelled by righteous indignation we took them apart. No mercy was shown. When one went down we piled in, a dozen or more at a time, kicking and stamping like men possessed. Although there were a lot of bizzies around, they could do nothing to stop us. We were fucking hyper and we left Oldham bodies all over the street.

Since then, surprisingly enough, we have become friendly with the Oldham mob. In fact we even hired coaches and went down there to help them take on the likes of Everton, Millwall and Huddersfield.

We never let a grudge get in the way of a good set-to.

*

Pre-season 1989/90. Once again the club had arranged a little tour of England. This time we would be going to Hull, Burnley and Aston Villa. The trip saw me at my organisational best. A Transit van had been hired to take twelve of us down south and, as usual, I was here there and everywhere making sure it all went smoothly. I took the names, collected the money for the hire and petrol, furnished the van with mattresses and pillows from my flat and even volunteered to drive. If I say so myself I looked after those boys better than their mammies ever could.

It was one hell of a journey. Have you ever been in a van with eleven other guys, all of them drinking copious amounts of beer or smoking hash, or both? The odours coming from the back were interesting to say the least. It was slow progress because we had to stop at every motorway service because the boys needed to pish or had an attack of the munchies. Strangely enough, given the racket in the back, I almost fell asleep when we were just outside Hull and it was only Cazshie shaking me with a 'waken up' that saved the day.

The game was at Hull's old stomping ground of Boothferry Park and when we arrived we thought 'what the fuck' and marched into the end occupied by the home support. Although we didn't spot the Hull mob we did see a few Hearts boys there. What they were doing there I have no idea but when they went for a slash we followed them into the toilets and battered them. That alerted the cops, who escorted us off the home terracing and into the away end.

After Hull we were due to play Burnley the next night, so we piled into our Transit vans and headed west to Lancashire. Not having the money for a hotel we slept in the back of the van, which is something I wouldn't recommend to anyone who likes home comforts or hates the smell caused by six boys dropping their guts after a night on the bevvy. I recall that another vanload of CCS joined us in Burnley, which boosted our numbers to around twenty, not nearly enough to take on a home mob of any real size. We spent most of the day in the pub and by the time we left to walk to Turf Moor some of us were the worse for wear.

Girvan was steaming – no surprise there – and because of his staggering and stumbling he gradually fell behind our little column on the trek to the stadium. Then, out of nowhere, there was a roar. It was Burnley, about fifty of the cunts. They were big guys, generally older than us, with an age range from early twenties to early forties. Girvan was closest to them and instead of rejoining us he ran straight at them. It wasn't Dutch courage. He would have done exactly the same if he had been sober. We could see him throwing punches for all he was worth. The trouble was he was so drunk that none of them were connecting. Given how badly outnumbered we were – and taking into account the size of their boys – we realised that a kicking was on the cards if we engaged. But we had to do something or Girvan would be an ambulance case. Within seconds the two mobs were going at it good style. Although after the initial skirmishes they were starting to get the upper hand our luck was in that day. The cops were quick to arrive and they managed to separate us. We then got an escort to the ground.

After two non-events we hoped for better things in Brum. We had returned home after Walsall but came back down in numbers for the Villa game, which was on 5 August 1989. Like the previous year at Oldham I reckon about two hundred of us headed down in cars and minibuses. We chose to go by road because after Oldham the previous year we knew the cops would be keeping a close eye on the trains. We met up at a motorway service station on the M6, just north of Birmingham, and drove convoy fashion into the city, where we parked outside an ice rink. On the way to the ground we looked for Villa but they were nowhere to be seen. Then when nothing happened during the game we got that sinking feeling. We would be going back to Edinburgh without having thrown a punch in earnest.

But we did get a fight that day. In fact we got two, although neither involved Villa. As we left the stadium right there in front of us was a mob of about eighty lads, three-quarters of whom were black. It was Birmingham City's Zulus, a formidable firm by any standards. One of them couldn't help himself. He gave us a mouthful of abuse, which sparked things off big time. Although they were strapping boys, and very game, our superior numbers soon told and we chased them. But our triumph was spoiled by the Birmingham bizzies, who were quickly on the scene to break things up. For some reason I was arrested, along with several other CCS, dragged into a van and taken to the station.

The police charged me with affray, kept me in for a few hours and let me go pending a court appearance at a later date. Meanwhile the rest of the CCS, having seen off the Zulus, got into another ruck at the ice-rink car park. After insults were exchanged with a few locals an ice-hockey team in full uniform piled out of the building and attacked our boys. The hockey guys were certainly no mugs and they put up a great fight but they still got a kicking and with the job done our lads decided to have a bit of fun. It was a trick that we often used on the Weegies back home and involved trading on Edinburgh's reputation as the smack capital of Britain. One of our guys, a diabetic, whipped out a hypodermic needle, stabbed one of the cunts in the arm and shouted:

'I'm a fucking junkie fae Edinburgh and youse have now got Aids. I hope you've made your last will and testament.'

I am told the ice-hockey man was shiting himself and that kept the boys amused on the long drive back to Scotland.

A few weeks later I had to come back down to Birmingham with another of our boys for a court case, at which we were represented by a woman lawyer. Although I am something of an expert on the Scottish criminal-justice system I knew fuck all about England's. It turned out that we didn't have to plead guilty or not guilty. We were bound over to keep the peace by the magistrate – apparently we agreed to it – which meant we were not convicted of a criminal offence. There was no jail time or even a fine. I was bemused but who cares? It was a result. Maybe we should adopt some of those good English practices in Scotland!

*

If our forays into England during the late Eighties had been of mixed quality – some good, some bad – all that changed in 1990. That was the year we won the lottery and the pools. That was the year we faced Millwall. At Millwall.

The London firm had a massive reputation in hooligan circles. Their stadium, the Den, was in the east end of London, in Bermondsey, a tough, working-class area strongly associated with the London docks. So it is no surprise there was a mob to match. On home turf they were damn near invincible. They had to be good. There were so many formidable mobs on their doorstep, mobs attached to clubs much bigger than Millwall. Think of West Ham's Inter City Firm, Arsenal's Gooners, Chelsea's Headhunters. But Millwall were, at the very least, the equals of any of that lot. They were just hard cockney bastards, boys who lived for a Saturday and the grief that came with it. Just like us.

We were about to enter hooligan heaven.

As usual I was heavily involved in the planning and logistics. In fact it was me who hired the two buses that were to take us down to London. To keep the Old Bill off guard one of the buses was hired from a company in Haddington, East Lothian, the other from a firm in Auchtermuchty, Fife. Being suspicious bastards the police would no doubt have checked with hire companies in Edinburgh. The game was on a Friday evening, 17 August, and our intention was to drive overnight from Edinburgh on the day before the game, which would get us into London early on the Friday. We met up in our spiritual home, the Royal Nip on Easter Road, at about eight o'clock on the Thursday for a quick drink. By the time we got a few beers inside us the excitement was at fever pitch.

Then we were hit by a bombshell. Of Hiroshima proportions.

The cops walked into the Nip and informed us they knew all about our plans. All our careful planning had been for nought. We were devastated. It was like the Scum snatching a last-minute winner in the Edinburgh derby. The cops had already told the two bus drivers they were going nowhere and to take the buses back to their garages. They informed us the fun was over and to get our arses back home.

After we had recovered from the initial shock we just thought, 'Fuck that. We have been planning for Millwall for weeks and we are not going to let the Old Bill mess it up.' There and then we decided we would get to London by hook or by crook. Some boys flew down; others went by car or train. We were determined not to pass up the opportunity of a lifetime. It was Millwall or bust.

I went home from the Royal Nip and got into a right barney with a gang of Dunfermline boys in a nightclub, an event that led to our attack on the Kronk a few weeks later. It meant that I didn't get to sleep until half three in the morning but I still managed to drag myself out of bed and along to Waverley for the six o'clock train to King's Cross. We arrived in London about four in the afternoon and made our way to a pub called the Hog and Pound, which is near Oxford Street. On our way we kept bumping into more and more CCS. Despite the best efforts of the bizzies it seemed that we would have a fair-sized mob after all, which, given Millwall's reputation, was just as well. When we arrived at the pub there were about eighty of us there and more arriving by the minute. It was a carnival atmosphere. Beers were sunk, songs sung and promises made about what we were about to do to poor old Millwall.

Then it was time to leave. We got the Tube and despite advice from a West Ham boy we had met in the Hog and Pound we decided to walk along the Old Kent Road, the spiritual home of all things Millwall. This was considered a no-no by other firms. It not only offended the home mob but also made you highly visible to their spotters. But we didn't want to sneak in. That wasn't our style. We didn't give a fuck if Millwall saw us or if it gave them a tactical advantage. We were proud of our team and proud of our mob and we were fucked if we were going in through the tradesman's entrance.

As it happened Millwall didn't spot us on the Old Kent Road. Maybe they weren't expecting us to come down from Scotland on a Friday night for what was, after all, a friendly. So far so good. Then, about half a mile from the Den, we spotted it, Millwall's boozer, the Crown and Anchor.

Bingo. It was time to make a name for ourselves.

The chant of 'CCS, CCS' went up, which they must have heard because as we got closer to the pub about thirty of them came out and took on our advance guard, which I am proud to say I was part of. They were big, hard-looking bruisers, generally older than us, with an average age of about thirty. I could tell at a glance why they were feared and respected by mobs from Exeter to Carlisle.

The fighting, while it lasted, was vicious. One false move against those guys and you would have ended up in hospital for a very long time. They were formidable but when our boys further down the road got into the action our superior numbers soon began to tell. We pushed them back, right into the pub, where they tried to make a stand in the doorway. In the meantime some of our boys had picked up plant pots from the pub garden and were hurling them through the windows. Other boys were turning over cars, which set off the security alarms. It was total fucking mayhem.

I vividly recall that one of their guys, a tall dude with long hair and a wild expression on his face, got a real doing. The shirt was torn from his back and then insult was added to injury when someone ripped his poncey gold chain off. Medallion Man then got a right kicking from a few of us before he was able to scramble back inside the Crown and Anchor. Serves the cunt right for having such bad taste.

Then, inevitably, we heard that familiar refrain: the sound of sirens. We scarpered, but the cops gave chase, rounded us up and escorted us to the Den. Some of us went in – including me – but others stayed outside, chatting about what we had just done. That was the wrong decision. Millwall saw their chance for revenge and attacked. They didn't discriminate between CCS and scarfers. In their eyes both groups were fair game. We could see what was going on from inside the stadium and we tried to break through an emergency exit to help them. But the cops pushed us back with their truncheons and we had to stand and watch as our mates and the scarfers got battered.

The game itself passed without incident. There were the usual songs from either side. We chanted:

We thought you were hard,
We were wrong, we were wrong . . .

They were going ape-shit. They couldn't get at us but they launched volley after volley of missiles in our direction throughout the ninety minutes. And they let us know in no uncertain terms what they were going to do to 'you Jock cunts' at full time. When the final whistle sounded the cops locked us in and when they did open the gates, about half an hour later, they thoughtfully provided us with an escort. The fact that there were dozens of Old Bill waiting to take us back to the Tube station shows you just how desperate Millwall were to get in about us.

As well as being out in force the cops thought it necessary to reconfigure half the road network of east London. Street after street had been blocked off to stop the locals exacting revenge. As we were walking we could see Millwall on every corner and this time they were well and truly mob-handed. Clearly, they did not appreciate being turned over on their own patch and they were baying for blood. To be honest if it hadn't been for the police we would have most likely got a real kicking. There were just so many of them and they were a great firm. Apologies for the cliché but we really were in the lion's den.

That was effectively how the night ended, although we did spend a fruitless few hours looking for other London firms to fight. On the train back home we reflected on our encounter with Millwall and pronounced ourselves well pleased. We had taken them on, on their own patch, and not been found wanting. It had done our self-confidence and our reputation the world of good. Other mobs certainly thought so. In fact, Millwall's main local rival – West Ham's Inter City Firm – put a notice in the London evening paper, the *Evening Standard*, congratulating us on a job well done. It was high praise from a genuinely top-class mob.

It was perhaps inevitable that someone would have to pay the price for what happened that night. Bobby Lipscombe was one of the main casualties. He was arrested and charged and charged with affray, for which offence, if memory serves me right, he got two-and-a-half years. I went down to London to give evidence at his trial, as did other members of the CCS. We were desperate to help Bobby but it was a gesture that the judge did not appreciate. His attitude was along the lines of 'how dare you bring these convicted hooligans down here as character witnesses or to give evidence that Mr Lipscombe was not involved in the violence'. So we probably did Bobby more harm than good.

The next time I saw him was in Glenochil prison. I was doing time for the Kronk and Bobby had been transferred back to Scotland on the so-called Gravy Train.

*

We fully anticipated trouble at Millwall. We didn't expect it at Telford, where Hibs were due to play a pre-season friendly on 18 July 1998. I didn't even know Telford had a football team, much less a mob. Our first problem was finding the place. In fact Telford, as we discovered, is about thirty miles north-west of Birmingham. By the late 1990s of course the casual movement was a shadow of its former self. Mobs were smaller, fights were rarer, the Old Bill had a firmer grip. That, and the fact we were playing a non-league side, meant that a minibus and a few cars were big enough to accommodate the forty or so CCS who made the trip.

I took the wheel and we drove through the night to Telford, arriving in the early hours of the morning. When we got there we found the local swimming baths and went for a quick dip and a shower. Then it was time for breakfast and a quick look round the shops before the pubs opened. After a couple of hours in a town-centre boozer we left and made for the supporters' bar attached to Telford United's ground. By scouting around we found a way of getting into the stadium without paying. It was simple: we kicked in a fire door and sneaked in.

We had taken up a position behind one of the goals and were leaning against the terracing wall, enjoying the summer sunshine. We really weren't looking for trouble but as usual it had a way of finding us. It started when a burly local pushed between me and Kev Wood. I could tell by his body language that he was agitated and ready to throw punches.

'This is my space. This is where I stand,' he informed us.

'Not today it's not,' I responded.

The red mist descended.

I stuck the head on him. The sound as my forehead met his mouth was very satisfying. Like the door of an expensive car being closed. He fell to the ground and I jumped on top of him, fairly pummelling him with my fists. Then more of their boys arrived and all hell broke loose. In the melee there was one very funny moment: Ged, one of our boys, was pissed out of his mind and when he tried to punch an opponent he swivelled right round and fell on his arse. The police were quickly on the scene, and, after they had separated us, Telford were escorted to the other end of the stadium.

Nothing else happened during the game but we did get a phone call to say that one of our guys, Davie McGrannigan, who had stayed in the pub with four other CCS, had been stabbed. As soon as we heard this news we left the ground and made for the town centre. It turned out he hadn't been stabbed although he and his four companions had been given a real going over by twenty Telford. Needless to say we put that right and ended up chasing Telford all over their own town centre.

*

The only other major foray into England came in July 2003. Once again we were going to the north of England and once again we were going to a crap town. In this case, Preston. We planned to take a huge mob down, for old time's sake as much as anything else.

For my part I was lucky to be on the trip. In January of 2003 I had been arrested along with ten other CCS for fighting with Rangers after being identified on closed-circuit television. Our case came before Dundee sheriff court just a few weeks before the game against Preston and with my form I fully expected to be remanded or given very restrictive bail conditions. The sheriff didn't remand any of us but he stipulated that our bail order would mean signing-on every Saturday at the local cop shop, or, for me and one of the Rangers boys, that the police would come to our houses on a Saturday to check up on us. (As usual I was singled out for special treatment.)

It meant we would miss Preston and potentially the biggest CCS tear-up in years. That would have been unthinkable so, thinking on our feet, we told the sheriff we were either away on holiday or taking a weekend break when the Preston game was on, and he lifted the bail conditions for one day only.

In the end it was an anti-climax. We took down two hundred to Preston, including most of our top boys. But their mob wouldn't play ball. They didn't come near and the only trouble came when a few of our guys broke away and fought some of them in a market. The next year I met a Preston lad in Tenerife and he said he couldn't believe the number of CCS that had travelled.

We got some consolation a week later when we played Sunderland at home. I was of course under house arrest that day and couldn't go but there was a tasty scrap with the Mackems outside the North British hotel, a scrap, I am told, that Sunderland, with a much bigger mob, won.

So how would I sum up mobs from south of the border? In a word: overrated. We always gave at least as good as we got against them, despite often being outnumbered. My only regret is that, Millwall apart, we never got to face the cream of English firms on a regular basis. They would really have tested our mettle.

But that is part and parcel of being a Hibby.

19

THE AULD ENEMY

It was unforgettable. There were thousands of saltires flying over Wembley. We had taken over the whole stadium. The cross of St George? You were more likely to see an Irish tricolour at a Rangers–Linfield game. It got even better after the final whistle. We fucking wrecked the pace, ripping down goalposts and digging up turf. Next time, I thought, I'll have some of that.

I had been watching the England versus Scotland fixture of 1977 on television. To a football-crazy boy of twelve there was no finer sight. We had taken on the English in their own backyard, soundly beaten them and claimed the home-international championship for the second year running. Wembley 1979 couldn't come quickly enough.

As the game drew ever closer I realised there was one insurmountable problem. My dad. He had reluctantly allowed me to go to Hibs games, home and away, but only because he knew I was being well looked after by older supporters. But a 14-year-old travelling to London was a different story.

'You're not going. You're too young. And that's final,' he told me, on what seemed like a daily basis.

It went in one ear and out of the other. I wasn't in a mood to listen. Wembley had cast its spell.

My pal Kano and I took the monumental decision to skive off school on the Friday, which was the day before the game, and make the great trek south. We couldn't afford a cheap bus ticket, never mind the train. So we hitch-hiked. After five separate lifts we got a stroke of luck at Scotch Corner. A friendly lorry driver picked us up and took us all the way to London.

We ended up at King's Cross. It was now five in the afternoon and I knew dad would be worried sick when he got home from work and found I had gone awol, although he would probably have a fair idea of my whereabouts. I phoned home, doing my best to put his mind at rest.

'Where the hell are you?' he asked, his voice a mixture of anger and anxiety.

'I'm at King's Cross.'

'How many times did I tell you that you weren't to go? London is full of dodgy people.'

'Dad, I'll be all right,' I said in my most reassuring tones.

Putting aside the run-in with dad – who grounded me when I got back home – it was a great weekend. A total eye-opener. The Scots took over not just Wembley but also the whole city. Despite the result – we lost 3–1 – there was no better feeling. I would be back for more.

My next trip to Wembley was not quite so innocent. It was now 1983. There were still no football casuals in Edinburgh but there was a thriving hooligan element made up of skinheads like me and other boys who liked to put it about at the football. So when I got to London I met up with around fifteen likely lads. We had a vague notion about taking on the English mobs but I am not sure exactly what we were expecting. To be honest we didn't have a clue, let alone a plan. Our minds were quickly made up when we saw the size of some of their club mobs. They were light years ahead in both size and organisation. There was no chance. We would have been slaughtered. When we got home we told our pals it would take something special if we hoped to be competitive next time round.

The next two England games were both at Hampden so the next chance we had to go to Wembley was in 1986. By now the CCS was Scotland's leading mob, ready and willing to take on the best that England could throw at us. I nearly missed the fun that year. I hadn't been able to get a ticket – they were like gold dust at that time – and so on the Friday night, on the eve of the game, I found myself at an engagement party with Margo.

HIBS BOY

As the night wore on and the drink started to flow my pals started to egg me on. 'You're not going to miss Wembley and fighting the English? It'll be great,' they said. I didn't need much persuading and around ten we made the decision to go. The only problem was transport. There was only seventeen hours until kick off. So one of my pals, John Dunlop, said he would do the decent thing. He 'borrowed' his dad's car.

Four of us were in the car and as we hurtled down the M1 we were full of the joys of spring until, that is, reality set in. It suddenly hit John. He had taken his dad's car without his knowledge and he was now four hundred miles from home. He just wanted to get back home with the car in one piece so he dropped Tam Hamilton and me off in Enfield and drove back to Scotland with Gals, the fourth passenger, for company.

We got a train into central London and made our way to Trafalgar Square. Along with the thousands of other Scots there were about sixty CCS in the square, drinking and playing football. We ran into casuals from other firms, including Celtic and Dunfermline. They were keen to join up with us and take on England. I managed to buy a match ticket and as three o'clock approached we jumped on a Tube and landed up at Wembley.

As usual Scotland fans had taken over much of the stadium but I noticed there were more English than usual. There was trouble right from the word go. With some of the CCS I was in the upper tier of the stand and it wasn't long before we were laying into England. Then, when that fight had been broken up by the cops, we saw other Hibs, Dunfermline and Celtic in the tier below getting it on with more English. In true SAS style we dropped down and joined the fray. The manoeuvre was captured for posterity by BBC and ITV, who both showed a clip of it on the national news. I was wearing a green-and-grey Rohan jacket (which I had nicked earlier in the week) and I can clearly be seen jumping from one tier to the next. I have a video of the broadcast and I still watch it amazed at how nimble I was in those days.

The fight with England was what I would describe as heavy duty. They were big, strong, beer-bellied thugs, older and more experienced than most of us. I remember dodging several haymaker punches, punches that would have knocked me out cold. These guys were not looking to take prisoners. I did manage to land a few blows before the cops moved in and broke it up, arresting me and a few others. I didn't go willingly and as they dragged me round the perimeter track I was doing my best to fight them off. Luckily for me half a dozen CCS saw what had happened and attacked the bizzies. That allowed me to break free and jump back into the stand. I knew my jacket was making me very conspicuous and so I took it off and handed it to a mate to put in his holdall.

Apart from the usual pleasantries nothing else happened during the game but we knew it would be a different story at full time. As we walked back to the Tube we ran into a big England mob. They were well up for it.

'Come in here you Jock cunts,' one said, gesturing to a multi-storey car park.

How could we refuse such a kind invitation?

Once again we only got a few minutes with England before the Old Bill arrived and split us up. In the confusion I got separated from the rest of the lads and ended up walking back to the station with a Celtic boy I knew. We were on the platform when about fifteen of the English we had been fighting with appeared at the top of the stairs. If it hadn't been for the crush of fans they would have been onto us in an instant. But we managed to jump on a train and were out of the station before they could get to the platform.

I ended up in Golders Green where the Celtic boy (who funnily enough was called Jock) had a bedsit. I phoned home and spoke to Margo.

'Where the hell are you?' she screamed. 'Everybody has seen you on the news. It has been on every broadcast.'

It turned out she had had dozens of phone calls to say that I was on the television news. She was convinced I had been arrested and refused to believe I was phoning from Jock's flat and not a police station.

I wanted to rejoin my CCS pals and so I got the Tube to Trafalgar Square. I found them but the problem was the sheer number of police. They had the place completely locked down. There was no chance of renewing hostilities with England.

We made our way back to King's Cross for the train. I slept all the way home, exhausted but happy.

By the time the next excursion to Wembley came around, in 1988, we had once again moved on. The CCS contingent was much bigger, at 120, and we had been in constant touch with other Scottish mobs in the run-up to the game. They would be coming from all over to take on England: from the Aberdeen Soccer Casuals, from Dundee Utility, from Celtic's Soccer Crew and even mobs from smaller clubs like Falkirk Fear and St Mirren's Love Street Division. Rangers of course weren't there. Knowing them they would have preferred fighting with the English.

So all in all I reckon there were around three hundred of us in Trafalgar Square on the Saturday morning before the match. We decided to take a walk, to reconnoitre, dividing into groups of fifty. Within minutes my group, which was mainly CCS, bumped into the opposition. It was Portsmouth's 6.57 Crew, a well known and highly regarded firm. After looking each other up and down for what could only have been a few seconds one of their front-liners shouted:

'What the fuck is this? Sending kiddies to do a man's job?'

Kiddies? We'll see about that.

There was a row of empty dustbins in the street. We picked them up and smashed right into Portsmouth. I grabbed one of their lads and threw him over a car bonnet, landing three or four good punches on his face. It seemed to be the same all over and it wasn't long before the 6.57 were on the run. So much for their big reputation.

That was just the beginning. As we turned the next corner we saw a bunch of the Tartan Army (from Dundee as we later found out) running hell for leather. They were being chased by a group of English casuals and when they saw us in front of them they must have thought they were trapped. I could see the fear written all over their faces. But when one of our boys roared, 'let's get intae these English cunts' they realised we were Scots.

As one man the CCS ran through the Dundee scarfers, piling into the English. With a real mob to contend with they weren't quite so confident and we soon got the upper hand. And fair play to the Dundee boys; some of them actually turned back and helped us take on their pursuers. Every little helps.

THE AULD ENEMY

It was unrealistic to suppose that we would have it all our own way. England had mobs from all over the country, mobs with a fearsome reputation. Mobs like the Chelsea Headhunters, who we also met up with that day. There must have been close to a hundred of them and as we flew in, fists flying, I knew we were in for a drubbing. And that's how it turned out. You just can't take on a firm of that calibre when you are outnumbered two to one. We must have faced about eight or nine English mobs. Some like Chelsea and Leeds got the better of us. That was hard to take, but understandable given their superior numbers. On a level playing field we would have more than held our own.

*

My only regret about England is that I wasn't able to face them in Scotland. They didn't often come to Hampden and when they did, as in 1989 for a three-nation competition that included Chile, I was in jail. That was a crying shame because the battle that year was truly epic, with huge numbers on either side. The CCS was of course in the vanguard, helping to harry the English all the way from the city centre to Mount Florida. The violence was ferocious: the English had come well tooled up and didn't think twice about slashing, stabbing or clubbing their immediate opponents. It was also widespread, with some skirmishes even taking place in Edinburgh when the English mobs from the eastern half of the country arrived at Waverley. There were 249 arrests on the day, provoking outrage in the media. Questions were asked in Parliament about how and why it had happened.

England's mob got the shock of its life that day. Their boys thought they would run our guys all over Glasgow. That was par for the course. They fancied themselves but in my opinion they were overrated. A lot of the mayhem they caused was drink fuelled and took place in little countries like Belgium and Luxembourg, which have no tradition of football violence. The English certainly looked the part, with their shaven heads and tattoos but it takes more than that. I am not saying they don't have some great mobs but so do we. A little less arrogance on their part would be very welcome.

In fact 1989 was the last in the series of Scotland's annual meetings with them so the next opportunity we got came seven years later. It was EURO 1996, which was being hosted by England, and the hype from down south was sickening. It was the 'Football's Coming Home' tournament, though what they had done to merit calling it that is beyond me.

Off the field the organisers prepared for mayhem. Not surprising given the reputation of some of the countries taking part. Apart from Scotland and England you had Holland, Germany, Italy and Turkey. There was a real frenzy in the media and in the run up to the tournament the papers were full of stories about casuals and other hooligans plotting battles both inside and outside the stadiums. It was said that London firms like Millwall, Chelsea and West Ham had threatened to join forces to take on the Jocks while we were putting together a Scottish supermob.

I was interviewed by many newspapers, desperate to find out what we had planned. The *Sunday Times* of 9 June 1996 reported that: 'Andy Blance is about to realise a lifelong ambition . . . he is going to represent his country deep in enemy territory for what could be the big one against England.' The paper went on to say that a gang of Scottish thugs – estimated at more than five hundred, of which I was one of the ringleaders – had bought tickets for the stand allocated to England's firm in order to mount an attack.

The *Sunday Mail* took the same line, explaining that 'hoodlum Andy Blance had boasted to [the *Mail*] about the hate-filled plot'. According to the paper we had decided to stay out of trouble at the Scotland–Holland game in case it put a fight with the English in jeopardy. Then, along with Girvan and Kev Peters, I was interviewed by Martha Kearney for BBC Television's flagship current-affairs programme *Newsnight*. It too reported that we were out to cause mayhem.

Of course we were desperate to get at England. We were sick to death of them mouthing off about what they were going to do to us and the Dutch and the Germans. Then there was their game in Dublin, against the Republic, in 1995. They were in the upper tier of the stand and had ripped up a few seats and thrown them at scarfers in the lower tier. That had got the game abandoned, which they somehow claimed as a great feat of arms. I'm sorry, but throwing plastic seats onto the heads of women and children isn't going to win you a medal for bravery. It was time to teach them yet another lesson.

Sadly, we never got it on with England. There were a few reasons. In the first place all the publicity had forced the cops to raise their game. The measures they put in place inside the stadiums were frightening. I went to the Scotland–Switzerland game as a spectator and was followed everywhere by a police spotter. At the England game I was in their end, having paid a tout £140 for a ticket. But there was no way I could do anything. It was lockdown. There were so many Old Bill there that you couldn't blow your nose without one of them offering you a hanky. Anyway, I was more concerned about what was happening on the pitch and like everyone else I was gutted when Gary McAllister missed that penalty.

The other problem was that the CCS was badly split by that time. James 'Fat' McLeod, once a loyal member, had formed the Scottish National Firm and he had taken quite a few of our boys with him. The SNF had set up camp in High Barnet, and had apparently arranged a major fight with England there, well away from the prying eyes of the police. Of course it never materialised and rather than kicking their heels quite a few of the SNF came down to Trafalgar Square to join up with us. Aberdeen were already there in good numbers, as were the Utility. There were also thousands of Tartan Army, singing and dancing and making a complete fool of themselves as usual. We didn't join in. We were too busy looking for England and with us to the fore, backed up by Aberdeen and the Utility, we did get into quite a few battles. But it wasn't as good as it should have been. The breakaway to the SNF and the farce that was High Barnet had seen to that. The worst of it was that some of the breakaway boys didn't learn and followed Fatty to Salou for the World Cup in 1998.

Some people just never learn.

20
BATTLES IN BRUSSELS

The CCS was in its prime between say 1985 and 1998. A few trips to destinations in Europe would have been nice, just to test ourselves against the best the Continent had to offer. Places like the Bernabeu, Rome's Olympic stadium, Paris St Germain. Hibs however only qualified for European football twice in that period: in 1989 and 1992, both times for the UEFA Cup, which was much less likely to throw up top opposition. I was in jail in ninety-two but I did get my first taste of European competition in eighty-nine.

It was some trip.

After beating Videoton of Hungary home and away we got FC Liege of Belgium in the second round. We drew 0–0 at home in the first leg and were confident of snatching an away goal in the return. But I would be lying if I said football was the main thing on our minds. We were determined to cause mayhem, CCS style.

We travelled to Belgium in groups of thirty, catching a train to London King's Cross and then one to Dover before crossing on a ferry to Ostend. Then it was onto base camp in the main square in Brussels, where around a hundred CCS mingled with several thousand Hibs scarfers. It was the day before the game and although it was early October we sat around that elegant square in our shirtsleeves, drinking and singing, without a care in the world.

It wasn't long before the trouble started. We got into running battles with a Heinz 57 variety of different groups: bikers, mods, Anderlecht's mob, local Moroccans. I am pleased to say we won most of those clashes but there was big trouble just around the corner.

When things had quietened down four of us decided to go for a walk to see a bit of Brussels. We were walking down a street that leads away from the main square when we came upon a group of five Moroccans lounging around a car. I sensed right away these guys were looking for aggro and sure enough, as we walked past, they went into their car and pulled out a sword each. They weren't toys. The blades were one-and-a-half-foot long and very sharp. I nearly shat myself; we all did. It was as plain as the nose on your face that these cunts were out to maim anyone who got in their way.

We didn't have any weapons with us so there was only one thing for it. We ran like fuck back to the square with the five Moroccans in hot pursuit.

Luckily, we got back to the rest of the boys without being slashed by the swordsmen. But we didn't get any respite. Around forty Moroccans arrived in the square and without so much as a by your leave attacked us. They were well tooled up so we had no option but to lift chairs, tables and bottles to fight them off. It was a short but extremely vicious battle in which boys on both sides were slashed, stabbed and bottled.

It was probably just as well the police were quickly on the scene, otherwise there could have been very serious injuries inflicted, or worse. The Moroccans backed off but we had nowhere else to go so the Belgian constabulary rounded us up and proceeded to bind our hands with little plastic ties. We protested our innocence, telling the cops that we had been sitting quietly having a few beers when we were attacked. It didn't wash. In fact they pulled out their guns and pointed them right at our heads. For the second time in less than half-an-hour I shat myself.

Then one of our boys, Derek Dykes, spotted that Girvan was still at it with the Moroccans:

'Girvan's fighting across the road,' he bellowed.

One of the cops thought that was a cheeky thing to do and hit Dykes on the bridge of his nose with a gun. There was a loud cracking noise that sounded like a bone being broken.

'That's fucking out of order,' one of our guys, Paul Dray, shouted.

His reward for sticking up for Derek was to get a gun poked into his ear. The cop did it with such force that he burst Paul's ear right open.

By this time the cops had bound about fifty of us with the plastic ties. They forced us to our knees before marching us off to the main police station where we were held overnight, twenty-five to a cell. I admit I was apprehensive. It was clear the gendarmes in this neck of the woods didn't fuck about and given that they were all packing guns I wondered what we were in for.

But then Tattie and Girvan appeared in the station, each of them being dragged by three cops. Girvan erupted, screaming abuse at his captors. Not to be outdone Tattie shoulder charged one of the gendarmes and bellowed: 'Watch where you're going ya fucking radge.' The cops just stood there and took it. At that moment we realised they weren't going to shoot us and that's when the party started. We sang all night long, played football with a rolled-up newspaper and set little fires. I think the cops were glad to see the back of us in the morning.

Word must have spread about what we had done because when we left the station there were a few Scottish journalists waiting outside. We were in no mood to cooperate and just told them to fuck off.

After a shower at our hotel we returned to the main square for a few beers, and we stayed there until it was time to catch the train to Liege. From Liege station we decided to walk to the stadium, which took us through a public park. There was a fairground there and Girvan, who was as usual half cut, stopped to buy a can of juice at a stall run by gypsies. (By the way he isn't an alcoholic; he just can't hold his drink.) The service was too slow for his liking so he started to mouth off at the staff. They answered him back, which raised the temperature by several notches. Girvan grabbed a coconut from the stall and launched it at one of the gypsies. He missed by inches but the gypsy bent down below the counter and brought out one of the biggest fucking knives I have ever seen in my life.

With the knife in his hand he came out of the stall and confronted us. I could see he was in the mood to inflict some serious damage. We pounded him with stones and bottles but by this time his mates from all over the fairground, also brandishing knives, appeared on the scene. Fair dos. We had invaded their territory and taken a liberty, now they were going to teach us a lesson.

There was nothing else for it. We bolted.

They came after us, about forty of the cunts. For the second time in twenty-four hours we were being chased by men with knives. It was one of the most frightening situations I have ever been in. These boys meant business and if any of us had been caught it would have been a slashing at the very least. Luckily, we could run faster than them and once we were out of the park they gave up the ghost.

Panic over we concentrated on tracking down Liege's mob. We didn't see them outside the ground and although some of us went into the home end we were quickly surrounded by police. So there was no trouble during the match, which Hibs lost 1–0, knocking us out of the competition. If we were to get to grips with a foreign mob it would have to be now because it might be years before the club was back in Europe. So as we walked back to the station we prayed that we would catch sight of Liege. We got lucky. At the top of a steep hill the Belgian bizzies tried to divert us. We soon found out why.

'You don't want to go down there. They are Liege hooligans,' we were told.

Whoosh. No sooner had the words left his lips than we were running headlong down that hill, right into the heart of their mob. It was a tasty scrap but, much to our disappointment, one that was quickly broken up by the Liege Old Bill. I was arrested again, for the second time on that short trip, and along with another of our boys I was taken to Liege police station.

In the cop shop we were put in a cell with three of the Liege hooligans we had just been fighting. We all had plastic ties round our wrists but one of the Belgians managed to free himself and then did the same for his pals. Chancing my arm, I asked him to free us as well but he just looked at me as if I was mad. I must have really got his goat because without further ado he smacked me right in the face. Despite being groggy from the punch I tried to head butt him but because I was still tied up I missed, lost my balance and fell onto the cell floor. The cops must have heard what happened because they came in and moved the Liege boys to another cell.

We were let out the next morning without charge. My only regret was paying in advance for my hotel room. If I had known I was to be a guest of the Belgian police for two nights in a row I could have saved myself £50!

As I said the next time Hibs got into Europe, in 1992, I was in jail. We had got there by winning the League Cup, a game I also missed thanks to prison. We were again drawn against a Belgian side, Anderlecht this time, and according to the boys that trip was if anything even more dangerous than Liege. Two Hibs fan, John McTigue and George Crook, both scarfers, were killed when they fell off the Edinburgh–London train near Huntingdon and then a CCS boy called Andy Tait got his throat slashed by Moroccans in Brussels. We were thankful he survived but I understand it was a close-run thing.

21

A MINI MAFIA

When you read some of the books written by casuals you think butter wouldn't melt in their mouths. They give the impression it was all just a youth cult, boys out for a fight and a good time. Others say they were attracted by the clothes and the music. I am not saying those things weren't important and I admit I am a bit of a fashion victim myself. But there was much more to it than looking good, having a scrap on a Saturday afternoon and listening to the right bands. At least there was for the CCS.

Whether people like it or not, for a period of four or five years, factions of our mob operated as a serious criminal gang. The CCS members I have mentioned elsewhere in this book weren't involved in these activities; they were just in it for a fight at the football. But, for many of the rest, there is no getting away from it. They were a mini mafia.

Drug dealing, mugging, assault, extortion, protection, arson, kidnapping, punishment beatings, shoplifting. The list is almost endless. In addition, at least five of our boys have been convicted either of murder or of culpable homicide, while others have done time for armed robbery, although to some extent these two crimes were things they did off their own bat rather than as CCS members. Nor were we the only ones. I know for a fact other mobs have dipped their toes into the waters of criminality.

It is time to set the record straight.

Drug dealing was the most common, and lucrative, activity. Although on a personal level it's not something I have ever done, mainly because

I hate drugs and the effect they have on people. In the early years of the CCS it was small scale and low key and so the sale of drugs was never a problem. It became one with the advent of the rave scene. Clubbers wanted to dance like dervishes all night long and there was only one way to do that. By swallowing Ecstasy tablets. I would say that 90 per cent of people at raves were on E, some taking up to a dozen tablets on a night out. That represented a huge market and the CCS did its best to meet the demand.

The business was done at venues all over the city of Edinburgh, without of course the knowledge or approval of the venue owners. The CCS turned up and started dealing, using their muscle to keep other dealers out. Ecstasy and to a lesser extent cannabis became big earners for the CCS. I would say that between 10 and 15 per cent of the boys were involved. However, while it was lucrative there was a major downside: the endless disputes over territories and customers. I can well remember different groups of CCS going after each other with baseball bats, swords and machetes. That saddened me and I did my best to act as a peacemaker when it kicked off.

There were other unfortunate consequences. Many of the boys developed links with dealers in other mobs, particularly the Rangers ICF, which seemed to have a considerable number of boys involved. The result was that they were reluctant to fight Rangers on a Saturday afternoon. To their way of thinking business came before pleasure, which was not something I could accept. To me the CCS was either a full-on mob willing to take on all comers or it was nothing. We also lost many boys to prison. When you get caught selling drugs the sentences are severe.

If drug dealing was a nice little earner extortion and protection weren't far behind. Licensed premises were a good source of income but shops were also on the list. I remember that the Baby Crew targeted two very upmarket clothes shops in Edinburgh. They walked in, bolted the doors behind them and filled black plastic bags with the latest fashions. The assistants saw it all but they were too scared to do anything. Calling the police was out of the question. They knew it was Hibs boys and that they would have got a doing after work. From the point of view of the shops it was little short of disastrous. With so much stock disappearing, their bottom line was being badly hit, so much so that one of the directors approached me.

'Look this will have to stop. I'll pay you to provide our security,' he pleaded.

So that's how I ended up doing the doors for two of Edinburgh's most fashionable shops. I brought in some older boys from the main mob and – surprise, surprise – the shoplifting was never a problem again.

If it hadn't been for the Kronk I could have cleaned up in the security game. I was offered four pubs by a major chain and a lot of other contracts besides. It was all because of the CCS's reputation. And for our 'customers' it worked. Troublemakers, knowing we were on the door, stayed away. Sometimes a pub would call us if there was a problem with rowdy customers. As soon as we walked in the trouble stopped immediately. It was less hassle than the cops and the licensing authorities never got to hear about it. So there was no possibility of a licence being taken away. Other pubs and clubs wanted nothing to do with us until that is we went in and trashed their premises. After that they were happy to pay us to stay away.

Our reputation was a big help in other ways. If someone was in a tight spot all he had to say was 'I am a friend of a Hibs boy' and he would be off the hook. It was that simple. Despite our fall outs over drug deals people knew we would always close ranks if we were threatened by outsiders. And that retribution would follow. Sooner or later we would get them.

Many of the mob had their own little operations going at that time. While I concentrated on providing security for shops other boys targeted pubs and nightclubs, taking fairly substantial sums for protection and the provision of doormen. They were what you might call 'freelance' operations, outside of the CCS core. But if they needed back-up the CCS was there, team-handed.

One group did try to take liberties. They were the doormen who worked for a company called Westland Securities, which provided security for many pubs and clubs in Edinburgh. One night some of their bouncers attacked two of our boys who were on a night out with their girlfriends. We were enraged. Having a go at boys who are out with their birds is right out of order.

Our retaliation was swift. We went to premises stewarded by Westland, beat up the doormen and trashed the place. They fought back; carloads of bouncers would cruise the streets looking for Hibs boys to attack. The feud intensified. We would do their bouncers outside a club; they would catch one of our boys on his own and give him a kicking. It was classic tit for tat.

A decision was taken to up the ante. One day some of the boys went to their office, tied up the two staff on duty and stole the personnel files. The CCS now had the names and addresses of all their doormen. They could be picked off one at a time. Around the same time we had the same problem with another security company. We didn't piss about with them either. One night a few of the guys went to their office and when they made sure there was no one inside, it was petrol bombed.

The feud with Westland finally came to a head one afternoon on the Meadows, a large, grass, common behind Edinburgh University. We had arranged to meet the doormen in a sort of winner-takes-all battle. They got the shock of their lives. When they turned up there were 150 of us lying in wait. One of the head honchos at Westland knew he had backed a loser and he quickly conceded defeat.

'That's it. We can't go on like this. I'll make sure my boys don't give you any more problems,' he said in a rather resigned tone of voice.

We accepted his assurances and let bygones be bygones.

*

At the peak of our power and influence our focus was not just on companies and commercial interests. Individuals were targeted too, although often in ways that made me uneasy. One such practice involved robbing casuals from other mobs for their clothes. Although the Baby Crew did most of the muggings some of the boys from the main mob were also involved. They used to watch for people leaving Edinburgh's trendy clothes shops with shopping bags and then they mugged them in the street, more often than not in broad daylight. There was no closed-circuit television in those days, making it much easier to get away with. On many occasions the helpless victims were even forced to give up the trousers and trainers they were wearing. It got so bad that people wore their work clothes to go shopping and carried Tesco or Safeway bags to put their purchases in.

Mugging was not something I ever got involved in. I dislike it for the same reason that I dislike housebreaking. It was too personal, unlike shoplifting, which is a crime against big business. There was another CCS activity that I had some concerns about. It wasn't something that was done for financial gain. It was strictly for a laugh, for the buzz. I am talking here about poof bashing,

I don't approve of homosexuality. To me it just isn't natural and I know the vast majority of CCS feels the same way. I know a few gay people, and I have to say they are as nice as the next person, but I still don't approve of what they do. So although I didn't join in the poof bashing I didn't have a great deal of sympathy for those who got duffed up.

In the early-to-mid 1980s poof bashing was a regular occurrence in Edinburgh. Sometimes there would be two CCS; at other times twenty would be on the prowl. They sneaked up Calton Hill in the dead of night, looking for homosexuals. When they found them they battered them senseless. The lucky ones managed to scuttle away, trousers and pants flapping around their ankles. Sometimes, I am led to believe, those who were targeted fought back but for the most part they just took their punishment. There was no question of police protection. In those days the Old Bill was probably even less sympathetic towards homosexuals than the CCS. How times have changed.

Despite my dislike of homosexuality, I never got involved in the poof bashing. You were targeting people who, by and large, couldn't fight back. They were civilians, non-combatants, and they should have been left to their own devices. But many of the boys refused to let it go. In fact they went on for several more years – until the inevitable happened. In the late 1980s a gay man was killed on Calton Hill and two of our mob were convicted of his murder. It brought a swift end to the CCS's involvement in poof bashing.

Murder of course is the ultimate crime and with hundreds of game, combative boys on the streets it was inevitable the CCS would commit its fair share. It just so happens that I had a front-row seat for the best known of them all. It was 1991, just months before I got my five years for the Kronk. I was working on the door of the Southside Snooker Centre in Edinburgh. I saw two guys who had just finished a game of snooker have a loud, drunken argument in the bar. One of them, by now in a real temper, cleared the glasses from the table in front of him with a sweep of his arm.

Unfortunately for him the glass landed at the feet of two CCS boys: Steven 'Tosh' Peters, who was 16, and Scott Moir, who was five years older.

On another day in another pub it would have blown over. But a throwaway remark from my fellow doorman as the two snooker players left the bar made that impossible:

'I think they threw that glass at you,' he said, without thinking, to Tosh and Scott.

That was it. Tosh and Scott leapt to their feet and went outside to look for the glass throwers. They cornered the two guys in West Preston Street and dished out a real doing. So frenzied was their attack that one of the victims, Stuart Bunch, a 26-year-old civil servant, was taken to hospital. After three weeks in a coma he died.

Tosh and Scott bolted before the bizzies arrived but they were later arrested and charged with murder. I was questioned about what had happened but told the cops I had seen nothing and so I wasn't called to give evidence. It didn't matter. At their trial in May 1991 Tosh and Scott were both found guilty of murder.

How did I feel about the man who was killed? To be honest I wasn't that bothered. That sounds harsh but I didn't know him from a cornflake and, let's face it, millions of people die every year and I can't mourn them all. The other thing is that I know Tosh and Scott didn't leave the club intending to kill Bunch. They just wanted to teach him a lesson. But like a lot of things we were involved in it got out of hand.

Our guys even faced problems in prison. One boy, Nelly, who had been banged up for a crime involving serious violence, was charged with the murder of another prisoner. As it happens he was innocent and the jury agreed when the case came to court, bringing in a verdict of not guilty. I am sure his membership of the CCS didn't help when the cops were looking for someone to pin it on.

Talk about giving a dog a bad name.

22
ALL THINGS MUST PASS

We knew it wouldn't last forever. At some point the CCS would begin to fade, to weaken, to become less of a player. And so it was that by the mid 1990s the rot had begun to set in. That is not to say we disappeared but our glory days had gone and they had gone forever. We weren't the only ones. Mobs all over the country got smaller and less active. Casuals just couldn't compete with the biggest mob of them all: the Old Bill.

I'll come back to the Old Bill later. But first there is the small matter of how certain members of the CCS did their best to break us up.

I think it started in 1991 after I got the five years for my part in the raid on the Kronk. I am not saying I was ever the leader of the CCS because we didn't have a leader. But I was one of the leading players and I did my fair share of organising. I booked buses, collected money for fines, reconnoitred away grounds on weekdays, planned ambushes, arranged meets with other mobs; you name it. I got so involved in the planning that the boys gave me a nickname: Gaddafi, after the Libyan leader who was so much in the news at the time. (If Colonel Gaddafi is reading this I hope he won't take offence at being compared to me!)

So when I was put away in 1991 it left a gap, one that others were keen to fill. Most prominent in this respect was James 'Fat' McLeod, a long-standing member of the CCS, who, with me and several others, was one of the accused at the Kronk trial although, unlike me, McLeod was found not guilty by the jury. To my way of thinking he has an over-inflated sense of his own worth but with me out of the way he came to the fore as a planner and organiser.

When I came out of jail in 1994, there was a power struggle for control of the mob, with me and likes of Girvan in one camp and Fat McLeod in the other. But I don't think that many of our boys rated McLeod that highly, either as a fighter or as a potential leader, and it wasn't long before he left for pastures new.

News reached us that McLeod had set up a new organisation: the Scottish National Firm. He had taken some CCS with him when he left and they had joined forces with boys from Rangers, Hearts and some of the smaller firms. To me it was a crazy idea, one that went against everything that casuals stood for. It drastically cut down the number of potential opponents they could face in this country. What did they plan to do? Go down to England every week looking for someone to fight?

There was no love lost between the CCS and the SNF. According to the *Daily Record* the SNF put a bounty of £5,000 on my head. Whether that is true or not I will never know but no one ever came looking for me. Then a vicious lie was put about that I was a grass, which in my book is just about the worst thing you can say about anyone. Apart from anything else look at the way the bizzies have treated me over the years. The thought of helping them turns my stomach.

It wasn't just lies we had to contend with. One night two members of the SNF – I don't know who they were – burst into McPherson's pub in Leith, where Girvan was drinking with some CCS pals. One was holding a gun, the other a knife. As my pal and a prominent CCS member Girvan knew he was the target, so he jumped up, ran to the toilet and locked himself in a cubicle. The SNF boys did their best to kick the door in but the bizzies arrived and nicked them.

After that things went downhill. There were many tit-for-tat incidents where we attacked them and they retaliated. On one occasion a dozen of them, all well tooled-up, turned up at Taylor's house and laid into him. In many ways it was sad to have former comrades at each other's throats.

The SNF didn't last for long. Without a firm connection to a club it was never likely to have the same emotional hold on its members.

When they disbanded its members joined a variety of other firms, including Rangers. The last I heard Fat McLeod was in Thailand trying to set up a property business. Although it collapsed the SNF had persuaded some of our best boys to join up. We could no longer claim to be the united family we once were.

The SNF was one thing, the Old Bill another. As I said it was the biggest gang of all, the one that had the most to do with our decline. Put simply they raised their game. A good example of their new, improved methods was our trip to Dundee in the late 1990s.

About 150 of us had gone up to Dundee by train, but on this occasion we had bizzies for company from the minute we left Edinburgh. Then when we got to the station the guard would open only one door, forcing us to walk through two columns of cops on the platform. We were frogmarched to a side door in the station and ushered onto two double-decker buses that had been hired by the Old Bill. The bus took us straight to the ground and then we were directed through another cordon of police to the turnstiles. After being watched for the whole ninety minutes we were sent back to the railway station using the same security procedures. There was no chance of anything going off.

It was clear that the cops were deploying more officers to monitor casuals on match days but this was backed up by a whole host of new measures. Closed-circuit television inside grounds was a nightmare for us. It meant individuals could be easily identified and targeted, whether during the game or at a time and a place that suited the cops. The police had also learned a lot about casuals and the top boys responsible for most of the mayhem. Most forces had intelligence officers, or 'spotters', who specialised in football hooliganism and they were able to brief their colleagues about known faces. At the same time the law itself was changed to make things harder for us and the introduction of banning orders, which could keep boys away from football grounds for years, was a particularly useful tool for the authorities. You know the old saying: you can't fight city hall. How true that is.

A perfect example of the bizzies holding a winning hand came at the Scottish Cup semi final of 2005, when we faced Dundee United at Hampden. I had arranged to meet Ralph Smith, one of the Utility's top boys, in Glasgow city centre so that we could agree on a venue for a little after-match barney. So there I was in George Square talking to my opposite number when, from just across the road, a plainclothes cop emerged from Gregg's the Baker and walked over to where we were standing. We recognised him straight away. He was one of Strathclyde Police's main football-intelligence cops.

'Andy Blance and Ralph Smith. What the fuck are you two doing here?' he spat, through mouthfuls of sausage roll.

Then they did a warrant check before sending us on our way with a warning that if we were seen talking to each other again we would be arrested. That wasn't our only problem. The cops knew which pubs the two mobs were in and had positioned dozens of officers outside. It was a virtual lockdown and so we didn't get to throw so much as a left jab that afternoon.

On a personal level I wasn't faring much better. I was served with a banning order in 2003 after my 'You Tube' fight with Rangers in Dundee. I did my best to get round it, even donning a wig and glasses to fool the cops. It worked for a while but eventually the bizzies got wise to it and I was out in the cold again. When the banning order was lifted things seemed to get even worse in terms of the attention I got. I remember an away game at East End Park when I was hauled out of the ground by the cops on the pretence of questioning me about an assault in the Ballroom nightclub in Dunfermline. It was shite of course. It was just their way of getting back at me for sneaking into games during the banning order.

That is all too typical of the way I am treated by the Old Bill today. I am still targeted, followed and spied upon from the moment I get anywhere near a stadium until the moment I leave for home. And so, of course, are the rest of the CCS boys, whether or not they are still active. I think the amount of time, effort and money the police have put into combating football hooliganism over the years is ludicrous. I am not saying we were angels but all we were doing was taking on other like-minded people. Boys from other mobs were willing participants, not victims. We were, and still are, monitored more closely than murderers or rapists, people who pick on innocent members of the public. I think it is because we were an easy target. The cops knew exactly where we were going to be and at what time. Catching serious criminals is obviously too much effort for the boys in blue.

It is little wonder that in the current climate there are only about six fights a season. Given our age – most of the original CCS are now in their forties – and the lack of new recruits I think we have witnessed the end of hooliganism as we once knew it.

And for the younger generation of hooligans that is a horrible thought.

23

ROLLING BACK THE YEARS

By the end of the 1990s and into the twenty-first century the casual scene was dying a slow death, despite the best efforts of diehards (like me) to keep it going. It meant, inevitably, that we saw less of each other. Many of the boys were now middle aged with the usual responsibilities that come with families, jobs and houses. They had become boring bastards who rarely had the time, money or inclination to travel all over Scotland looking for a fight. So any opportunity to get together was seized with both hands. We have always been close, and we still are. We will never forget what we achieved together as a mob.

That is why Bobby Lipscombe's suggestion for a group of us to apply to Sky Television's Saturday morning football show *Soccer AM* was a stroke of genius. If we could pull it off not only would we get on the telly but also there would be a weekend away in London for seven of us, paid for by Sky. It would be just like the old days.

This is how it came about. Hibs had a free Saturday on 2 September 2000 when Scotland were playing a World Cup qualifier in Latvia. Our immediate thought was: what the fuck were we going to do with no game to watch? We didn't fancy the long trip to Riga but we couldn't go without our football fix, even for one day. We put our heads together in the pub but after an hour of considering the possibilities we still hadn't come up with an answer. Then Bobby piped up with, 'What about *Soccer AM*? They have fans of different clubs on every week.' We all agreed it was a brilliant idea. Apart from anything else it was one of our favourite programmes. We gave thanks for Mr Lipscombe's moment of inspiration.

There was only one small problem. Persuading the programme makers to put us on. After all there were probably dozens of clubs who were desperate to take part. As it was Bobby's idea we got him to phone Sky and put our case. He did, and to his surprise he got through to Tim Lovejoy, the co-presenter.

'Why should we put Hibs fans on and not fans from another club?' Lovejoy asked.

'Because we're top of the league,' Bobby replied.

He was telling the truth. We were top of the league, a rare occurrence, but then the season had only just started. Whether that swung it we will never know but, whatever the reason, they accepted us. Of course they thought we were normal fans. There wouldn't have been a hope in hell if they had known they were about to have seven CCS descend on them.

The Magnificent Seven who travelled to London consisted of Bobby, Derek Dykes, Girvan, Bongo, Davie Graham, a boy called Darren (whose second name I can't recall) and me. We caught a train from Edinburgh Waverley on the Friday morning and got into King's Cross around five in the afternoon. Apart from Bongo and I – the two teetotallers – the rest had been drinking all the way there. And they drank for two more hours in the pub we found close to the station. So by the time we got to our hotel in Bethnal Green most of them were already steaming, although it didn't stop them buying a very large carry-out before we got on the Tube. One or two of the boys had also been smoking dope and were even more blitzed than the rest. It was a beautiful hotel and at £200 per person per night it should have been. Not that we cared because Sky were picking up the tab.

The serious drinking started again after a very nice dinner. Before long it all came flooding back. We remembered the good times, the boys we had fought with, the victories and the defeats. We drank to Hibs, to the pals who were no longer with us, to the many good lads from other mobs. For me the CCS, first and foremost, had been about friendship and that's what outsiders never get. As we sat there reminiscing it made me realise just how wonderful those years had been and how much I missed them.

Then as I looked around the table something else hit me. I was in the company of some special people, people who mean such a lot to me. I will always be grateful for their friendship.

As the only teetotallers Bongo and I left the party about midnight and went up to the room we were sharing. Needless to say the other five carried on drinking until they were turfed out of the bar at God knows what time in the morning. But did that stop the party? Did it fuck.

The next thing Bongo and I knew was when the phone next to his bed rang at three o'clock. It was the night manager. He told Bongo that unless we kept the noise down the police would be called. Bongo told him to piss off, explaining that we had been fast asleep. But we knew where he was coming from. All we could hear from the rooms along the corridor were Hibs songs and loud voices cursing the Scum. I don't think the other five got a wink of sleep.

We got up around eight and when the curtains were opened we realised just how riotous a night it had been. There were dozens of empty bottles and cans on the hotel's beautifully maintained lawns and flower beds. I could just imagine the gardener's face when he saw the mess.

When we went down for breakfast, not surprisingly, the five of them were still paralytic. Girvan, of course, was the worst and from past experience I knew he would have to be watched closely. Fuck knows what the people at *Soccer AM* would think when they saw him. I said, 'You keep your mouth shut. I'll do all the talking this morning.'

A minibus arrived and drove us to Sky, a journey that took about twenty minutes. Outside the studios we stopped at a security gate. It was too much for Girvan.

'Hurry up. I'm bursting for a fucking pish,' he bellowed.

'Shut the fuck up or we won't get on,' I warned him.

The guard, perhaps reluctantly, let us in and we were shown to our dressing room. We were in high spirits, loud and raucous, pumped up with adrenaline. It was not unlike the feeling you get before taking on a rival mob.

Then a production assistant appeared with an armful of Hibs tops. They were the new white away strips and had been sent to Sky by the club for us to wear on the show. Hibs must have thought we were scarfers because they wouldn't have taken anything to do with a bunch of CCS.

ROLLING BACK THE YEARS

It was at that moment that Helen Chamberlain, the other co-presenter, came in to say hello. She was fit, and down-to-earth with it. As we changed into the tops she looked closely at the Hibs tattoos that adorn my upper body and asked me where I had them done. She said that she had a tattoo but couldn't show us because it was in an embarrassing place.

'Come on. Let's see it,' I said.

The others joined in, egging her on to show the tattoo. So she hitched up her skirt, revealing a thong and a very shapely arse. But then we saw the best bit. There, tattooed on one milky white cheek, was the club crest of her team, Torquay United. She was a great sport, someone you warmed to immediately. Unfortunately, I didn't feel the same way about Tim Lovejoy. I thought he was aloof, in my eyes a bit of a snob, not someone I would like to spend time with.

In the lead up to the show, which goes out live, it became clear that the producers were concerned about how we would behave on air. In fact they told us we would have to tone it down. There was a fat chance of that. It was time for the CCS to behave like CCS.

There were always players on *Soccer AM*. Today it was Steve Bull, formerly of Wolves and Ade Akinbiyi, who, I believe, played for Leicester City. There was also a band: Reef, if memory serves. But there was no danger about who would get all the attention. From the minute they started broadcasting we were chanting 'CCS, CCS' at the top of our voices and we kept chanting for almost the whole show, alternating the CCS chant with 'top of the league' and other ditties in honour of Hibs.

There is a little sequence in which the group of fans is interviewed by Tim Lovejoy. He asked me what I thought of Hearts and I told him.

'They are the only form of life that looks up to the gutter.'

'You can't say that on live television,' he replied, taken aback.

'There's not much we can do it about it now. I've just said it.'

That wasn't all. About two-thirds of the way through I took off the Hibs top and revealed to the camera what I had on underneath. It was a T-shirt with a slogan that reads: 'CCS. Licence to Swagger'. Bobby followed suit. His T-shirt had the CCS mottoes: 'These Colours Don't Run. Hibs Casuals on Tour' and the green-and-black Union

Jack that we got made up to annoy Old Firm fans. Because the show was live the producers were powerless to stop us.

After the broadcast we filed into a social club that was attached to the studios where we enjoyed yet more free drink. One of the regular characters on the show, Rocket, came over for a chat and he said that Sky had been inundated with complaints from viewers upset that known hooligans had been invited on. It turned out they had never had so many e-mails and phone calls about any of their shows.

Helen Chamberlain also came along for a drink although I didn't see Lovejoy anywhere in the room. To me Helen didn't seem in the least bit upset about what had happened. I am sure she would never condone violence but she thought we were great – boisterous but passionate, like real fans should be.

Our appearance on *Soccer AM* got us noticed by the *News of the World*. A reporter phoned Bobby and asked about our appearance on the show and also about past exploits. Bobby was happy to oblige and he even said we were considering causing trouble at an England game being played at Wembley that afternoon. It was all crap of course but the paper lapped it up and we got a big spread the next day.

We got our train back to Edinburgh, tired but elated. Weekends don't come much better than that.

24
REGRETS? I HAVE A FEW

I am happier and more content today than I have any right to be. I own my own house, run my own business and am close to my family. I am also in a serious relationship with an attractive, intelligent woman. Given my previous exploits I must be one of the luckiest guys in Scotland.

I still live and work in Inverkeithing. I bought my council house five years ago. Although the flat is not in what you would call an upmarket area it is all mine, and, if I say so myself, it is well decorated and nicely furnished. I go on holiday abroad every year and more importantly I follow Hibs home and away and have a good social life. All in all it is a great lifestyle.

Despite my past I am now a legitimate businessman, although some people do compare me to the *Minder* character, Arthur Daley, or to Del Boy in *Only Fools and Horses*. The main difference is that I don't need a Terry McCann to sort out geezers who take liberties.

I run two businesses in Inverkeithing. One is a sunbed shop, Sunshine on Fife. The other, which is next door, is an internet cafe and has just opened for business. The sunbed shop does well in the summer but trade tends to drop off in the winter. Hence the internet venture. In addition I buy and sell anything that will turn a profit (apart of course from drugs): for example seasonal goods like fireworks in November or Christmas decorations. I often sell on tick, but I don't charge interest. I am not into taking advantage of my customers. Inverkeithing is a working-class town and many people are not well off. But I do expect them to honour their side of the bargain by paying me on time.

Living in Inverkeithing suits me. After all it is only ten miles from my beloved Easter Road. I know everyone in the town and they know me. They accept me for what I am, a sort of local boy made bad! Many of them are not only customers but also friends. I try to give something back to the town and in recent years I suppose I have become a kind of unofficial neighbourhood warden. I am talking here about anti-social behaviour. I won't stand for it and thanks to my reputation it is almost unheard of round our way. If I didn't do it no one else would. The council and the Old Bill don't give a toss about people like us.

One of the most annoying – and dangerous – practices that I have tried to stamp out is speeding cars and buses. Where I live there are lots of young kids, many of whom play in the street. For the life of me I can't understand why drivers insist on doing speeds in excess of 50 miles per hour on our estate. In 2006 a child was knocked down and killed just a stone's throw from my house.

Do they really want to kill another one?

I often stand in the middle of the road and stop speeding cars. I then give the drivers a piece of my mind. They usually get the message. After all I've had some experience in getting my message across over the years! Such are my powers of persuasion that violence has only been necessary once and, as you might know, a bus driver was involved.

One day, about two years ago, a bus was hurtling down our street. He must have been doing sixty. There was a horde of kids playing football in the street, including my son Jack, who was then eight. I was in my car, heading for town, when the bus passed me. I saw how fast he was going but decided to let it rest and go about my business. But, as I drove, I got angrier and angrier.

I turned round and went looking for the driver. He was parked up for his tea break at the end of our street. He hadn't even been in a hurry.

'What was the need for the speed just now if you're not even in a hurry?' I asked, full of righteous indignation.

'What are you on about?' he replied, looking at me as if I was talking shite.

If he had given me a reasonable explanation I would have let it go. But the guy was being an arrogant prick, in true bus-driver style.

I just lost the plot, grabbed him by the throat and whacked him in the face.

Maybe next time he'll remember his Highway Code.

*

I am delighted that my family live close by. I am in touch with all of them. It is great that dad is only five minutes away. He has recently been ill and I like to think that I did my bit, along with my sisters and my brother, to help him with hospital appointments and the like. After all I have put him through over the years it was the least I could do.

I have three sons: Kevin (23) and Jamie (22) from my marriage to Margo and Jack (10), from a later relationship with a woman called Shona. That was another relationship that broke up due to my involvement with the CCS. Although things had quietened down considerably on the hooligan front by the time I got involved with Shona, I was still arrested on quite a few occasions. Quite understandably, it was something that Shona found it hard to come to terms with. The final straw was when I chose to go to London for *Soccer AM* rather than take her to an engagement party. We parted soon after.

I am pleased that I am still on good terms with Shona and that between us we are doing our best to raise Jack. Sometimes he stays with me, sometimes with his mum. The kid is a real livewire: outgoing, sociable, the life and soul of the party. I would like to say he is a chip off the old block but I don't want to ruin his prospects!

I am close to Kevin and Jamie, my two oldest boys. I brought them up in the faith; they are both fanatical Hibbys, just like their dad. Who was it said that the apple doesn't fall far from the tree? They are like me in another respect. Both are fully paid-up members of the football-hooligan brotherhood. Some people might think that their involvement in the family business makes me secretly proud. It doesn't. I didn't want them to follow in my footsteps and I worry constantly about what might happen. For that reason I always phone them after a game, just to make sure they are all right. I could have warned them off the hooligan game but I felt that would be hypocritical. When one of them got arrested I remember Margo pointedly asking: 'Where did he get that from I wonder?'

It is perhaps only in a crisis that we realise how much we love those closest to us. I remember when Kevin was twelve he had to get four teeth removed. We took him to a specialist dental surgery in Edinburgh, one with an operating theatre. I went into the theatre with him and as the anaesthetic was being administered I held onto his hand. As it took effect his eyes closed and his hand went limp. It is not easy seeing your little lad going to sleep under those circumstances and I am not ashamed to admit that I was in tears. I was just so relieved when he came to after a successful operation.

It has been tough for Kevin and Jamie and to a lesser extent for Jack. They see the newspaper articles describing me as a vicious thug, as do other members of my family. It can't be pleasant for them and I am sorry that they have to read that stuff. The older boys have also come in for special attention from the Old Bill at the football, simply because they are my sons. That is true of the sons of other CCS members. I am afraid it goes with the territory.

As I have already acknowledged my CCS-related activities have been very destructive in terms of my relationships with women. So I think I had resigned myself to the fact that any long-term attachment would founder for the same reason.

But I got lucky.

Kim came into my life in 2007. I first saw her in the Hibs supporters club next to Easter Road, where she worked as barmaid on weekends. I made discreet enquiries but was told that she was seeing someone else. That was that I thought to myself. But a few weeks later I bumped into her, asked her out on a date and before long we were an item.

Some people obviously thought I wasn't good enough for her. They would sidle up to her mum and drip poison into her ear.

'Do you know what that guy seeing Kim has done?' they asked her.

But she had an answer for them.

'As long as he treats my daughter properly and she is happy then I'm happy.'

Kim is one reason I have tried to stay out of trouble. There are others. I have three sons to think of and Jack after all is still just a boy. He needs me around. Going back to jail now would be unthinkable, a massive wrench for me and my family. I also have to accept that I am no longer the sprightly young thing who steamed into opposition mobs at the drop of a hat. That is a young man's game; it is not one for a man in his mid-forties.

I have done my best to stay out of trouble in recent years. Some people might not believe that but it's true. The problem is that, on occasion, my past catches up with me. For example at Tynecastle in January 2009 I went at it with four of the Hearts mob. It wasn't planned; they attacked me and I had to defend myself. I can honestly say that the only reason for me to come out of my self-imposed retirement would be if another Raymie Morell-type situation arose or if Hibs fans were getting a real doing. Nowadays I am more likely to phone up some of my old adversaries from other mobs for a chat. We reminisce for hours about the old days, like a couple of Chelsea pensioners talking about the war.

One thing hasn't changed. I am still as Hibs daft as ever. I go to every first-team game, home and away, and that includes pre-season games in Europe and the Inter-Toto Cup. I am also an occasional spectator at reserve fixtures and have been known to go along to youth-team games. If I say so myself there can't be many more dedicated supporters in Scotland than Andy Blance. So don't give me that crap about casuals not being real fans.

Looking back I can't say that I have no regrets. That would be foolish and arrogant. I deeply regret the hurt I have caused my family. It was particularly tough on dad, who tried so hard to keep me on the straight and narrow. He couldn't have done any more; in the end it was down to me and me alone. I also know that I could have had a good career or built up a much bigger business. I showed promise at school and even dad admits that I have always got on well with people.

While I am on the subject of regrets I would like to add one more. I am sorry for what I did to John Doherty, the man I hit with the axe outside the Kronk. I have met him a few times since then and I know now that he had nothing to do with the threats that were made against me and my family. In fact he is a pretty decent bloke.

With all that off my chest I can safely delve into my memories. Although I have now given up the hooliganism for good barely a day goes by without me recalling a battle we had or a boy I fought with. I miss the great days. We all do. The laughs, the shared dangers, the camaraderie, the adrenaline rush, celebrating our triumphs in the Royal Nip and the Penny Black. What I wouldn't give to be running full pelt at Aberdeen, steam coming out of my ears. With boys like Girvan, Tattie and the Welsh brothers at my back we couldn't lose. I pity the young fans of today. They will never know how close we were, the pride we had in our club and in our mob. Those days have gone and they are never coming back.

Long live the CCS.

MEN OF THE CCS

Ashy, John A, Dougie A, Mikey A, Jamie A, Rab A, A'body, Junior A'body, Fat Al, Beefy, Kevin and Jamie B, Johnny B, Cha B, Andy B, Martin B, Bego, David B, James B, Jamie B, Paul B, Gordon B, Banner, Charlie B, Belly, Bongo, Budgie, Ricky B, Brains, Darren B, Bubs, Ali C, Tam C, Pete C, Andy C, Kenny C, Crombie, James C, Rory C, Cazshie, Billy C, Toby C, Paul C, Fraser C, Cozzi, Connors, Cazshie Colin, Cheggers, Warren C, Catso, Clegi, Campbell, Derek D, Philly D, Paul D, Andy D, Billy D, Gogs and Dougie D, Mikey D, Andy D, Billy D, Shaun D, Lawrie D, Stu D, Ross D, Alan D, Dode, Johnny D, Vince D, Alan D, Dodgy D, Lee D, Dono, Dino, Sean D, Daz, Doc, Davie E, Eddie, English Steve, English Sean, Craig F, Scott F, Neil F, Darren F, Fergie, Neil F, Kev F, Greedy, Big Graham, Craig G, James G, John G, Scott G, Rab G, Adrian G, Gribble, Ged, Gozman, Gadge, Tam and Adam G, Gemmell, Horan, Jamie H, Stevie H, Kevin H, Hendo, Hoggy, Davie H, Dougie H, John and Mark H, Jardine, Andy J, Jam, Jamesy, Jimmy Jenners, Kinnoch, Keek, Kirky, David K, Ian K, Leif, Kenny K, Ivor L, Bobby L, Tony L, Duncan L, Davie L, John La, John Lo, Craig, Jack and Mark L, Scott L, Lawrence, Paul L, Fat McL, Willie McF, the brothers McA, Jim McM, Motion, Gary M, Mars, Meatbaws, Brendan and Jed McC, Eddie M, Keith M, Pete M, Raymie M, Marcus, Maxwell, Mow, Dougie Mac, Warren Mac, Scott M, Joe McG, McGrannigan, Brian Mac, Chris McC, Cammy McK, Darren M, McGeever, Phil M, Lee McK, McNulty, Scott M, Moyesy, Mashy, Mikey N, Nicol, Glen N, Martin N, Nelly, O'Hare, Ormo, Andy P, Ross P, Kev, Acky and Tosh P, Baz P, Paul from Winchburgh, Pancho, Pele, Tel Boy, Chrissy R, Graeme R, Bud R, John R, Richo, Tam R, Frank R, Davie R, John R,

HIBS BOY

Jim R, Cha R, Alan and Nicky R, Neil R, Rosano, Justin S, Colin S, Jim S, James S, Steely, Craig S, George S, Gogs S, Ricky and Gary S, Cammy S, Mark S, Smadge, Simmy, Soggy, Shanley, Skeets, Stanton, Teddy, Jamie T, Taylor, Andy T, Tycey, Mikey T, Titch, Toddy, Acky T, Tooly, Tiff, Tucker, Tottenham John, Tony Tesco, Tattie, Blair U, Stevie U, Ian W, Kirk W, Leon W, Mikey W, Stevie W, Kev W, Raymie W, Wickstead, Worzel, Sean and Brad W, Woody, Sean W (junior), Young Woody brothers, Scott Y, Geoff, Y, Zod, Zander.

I know I have missed some of you out. But after twenty-odd years I was never going to remember everyone. Let's all go now to Easter Road.

Pride in the club
Pride for the badge
Pride of the east

DAILY RECORD, Monday, August 15, 1994

THEY'RE BACK

ON THE WAY TO A MATCH ... football fans in trendy gear make their way to a Premier Division match with the police keeping a close watch for any trouble

By PATRICK HAINEY

Evil casuals threaten new reign of terror

THE ugly spectre of the football casual is bringing fear to the streets again.

On the first day of the new season, the expensively dressed thugs returned with a vengeance.

And police fear the menace that plagued the game in the 80s is back to stay after years of inactivity.

Battling casuals caused mayhem in front of horrified tourists and festival-goers in Edinburgh on Saturday.

Rival gangs of Hibs and Dundee United thugs met up for a pre-arranged fight in a pub on William Street.

And as police probed the violence, a spokesman said they were monitoring the situation "with considerable concern".

Asked if there was a possibility of further confrontations, he added: "There is a definite threat and we will be doing everything we can to combat it."

ECHOES

British Transport Police Inspector Kenneth Graham said: "This is new behaviour.

"You can go back two or three years to the last time we had any trouble with casuals.

"Any return to the levels of violence we had in the 1980s would be very worrying."

The Edinburgh incident echoes the horrifying violence of the 80s when casuals plagued grounds across the country.

Supt Adrian Appleby of the National Criminal Intelligence Unit said there was evidence some casuals had tooled up with firearms.

He warned: "We have not seen guns used in soccer violence - YET.

"But we believe leading hooligans have bought guns."

Drugs and neo-Nazi politics have also been a feature of the gangs.

FAN

The Lothian and Borders Police spokesman said: "These people blacken the name of every decent fan.

"I don't know what their game is - but it certainly isn't soccer."

TOLL OF THE THUGS ... shopkeepers in Edinburgh clean up the riot debris

BAN THESE VIDEO THUGS

A SCOTS soccer thug's video boasts have sparked a storm of outrage from football fans.

And one leading supporter has already called for the sick video Trouble on the Terraces, due to go on sale next month, to be banned.

The film, showing scenes of soccer violence from all over the world, includes an interview with an unnamed hooligan – who claims to be an Aberdeen fan.

The mystery lout spouts his neanderthal fighting philosophy and boasts of being a member of the fascist BNP.

Susan Scott, secretary of the Association of Aberdeen Supporters Clubs said: "I don't agree with it at all. Speaking purely personally I would like to see it banned.

"There is a danger that a video like this will lead to more hooliganism.

"I don't know who this so-called fan is, but we don't call someone who goes looking for trouble a supporter."

Ian Taggart, secretary of Aberdeen, said: "There isn't that much violence in Scottish football and I can't see why they would want to focus on the negative things."

Grampian police said they would deplore any video glorifying soccer violence.

A spokesman added the "intended arrest rate was "very, very low".

CITROËN AX

FREE INSURANCE

17-75 YEAR OLDS

PLUS DRIVE AN AX FROM ONLY **£79** A MONTH PLUS DEPOSIT AND FINAL PAYMENT **(8.0%)** APR

THE SPECIAL EDITION AX SPREE.
TWO GREAT DEALS ON ONE STUNNING CAR.

- 4 colours available – Cardinal Red, Curaçao Blue Metallic, Calypso Green Metallic and Tropical Violet Metallic, all with matching painted bumpers.
- Available in 3 or 5 door, petrol or diesel.
- All models feature stereo radio/cassette, sunroof, tinted windows and sports steering wheel fitted as standard.
- A range of attractive finance deals, including Elect 3, available.
- Free insurance applies to drivers aged 17 to 75.

Example: AX Spree 1.0i 3 Door	
Elect 3 price	£6,944.00
Deposit (30%)	£2,083.20
One payment on signing	£78.97
23 monthly payments (8.0% APR)	£78.97
Final payment	£3,615.00
Total payable	£7,593.00

ON THE ROAD FROM UNDER **£6,697** CITROËN elect 3

DISCOVER WHAT CITROËN CAN DO FOR YOU.
CALL FREE ON 0800 262 262 FOR DETAILS.

In the Eighties and Nineties, casuals in general were bogeymen for the tabloid press, even if the threat we posed to society was minimal. This story, from 1994, is about a clash we had with the Dundee Utility.

(courtesy Mirrorpix)

There was near hysteria about the possibility of casuals causing mayhem at Euro 1996. I even got interviewed by *Newsnight* in the run up to the tournament and also for this article in the *Sunday Mail*. I had some hair in those days!

(courtesy Mirrorpix)

GANG CHANTS: High Court jury told of Hibs Casuals link with pub trouble

RIOT TERROR PAIR JAILED

TWO MEN linked with a notorious gang of Hibs Casuals were today starting jail sentences totalling nine years.

A four-week High Court trial heard that chants of CCS — Capital City Service — were heard during a riot at The Well pub in Dunfermline last September 7.

The jury took five hours to convict Andrew Blance (26) and Ivor Levine (29) of mobbing and rioting, attempted murder and three charges of assault.

Lord Kirkwood told them their behaviour could not be tolerated in a civilised society.

Blance, formerly of Churchill Place, Rosyth, but now living in Edinburgh, was sent to prison for five years. Levine, of 20 Orchard Brae Gardens, Edinburgh, was jailed for four years.

Similar charges against Mark Lynch (20), of 11 Brougham Street, Edinburgh, were found not proven.

The court heard that one man, John Doherty, was critically injured when he was hit on the head and back with an axe or a meat cleaver. A policewoman fainted when she saw his injuries.

After the jury returned their verdict at the High Court in Dunfermline, Blance gave a thumbs-up to friends on the public benches. Levine turned to his father and girlfriend and shook his head.

Mark Lynch smiled at his tearful mother, Joyce Lynch, who said later that Mark and his brothers were all Hibs supporters. "They go to the games," she said, "but they're just like any other fans."

Saturday Evening News — Saturday, August 3, 1991 — Price 22p

The raid on the Kronk in 1990 was a turning point in my life. After the then longest trial in Scottish criminal history I was sentenced to five years in jail. It also led to the break-up of my marriage, enforced separation from my young family, the loss of valuable contracts in the security industry and to my demonization in the media. This story appeared on the front page of the *Edinburgh Evening News* at the end of the case.
(courtesy Scotsman Publications)

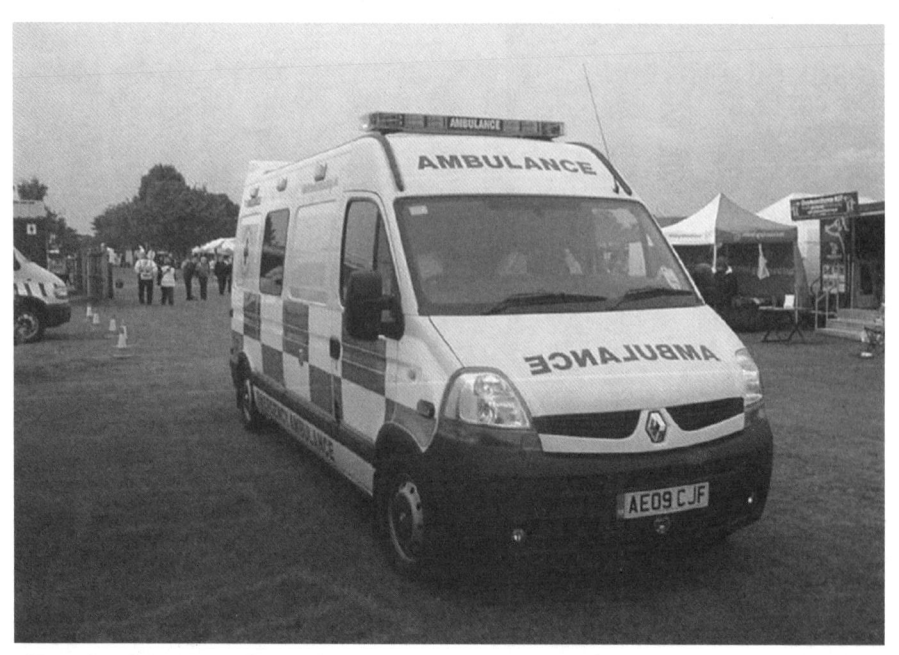

Taxi for Hearts! This is how the Scum usually went home after taking on the CCS.

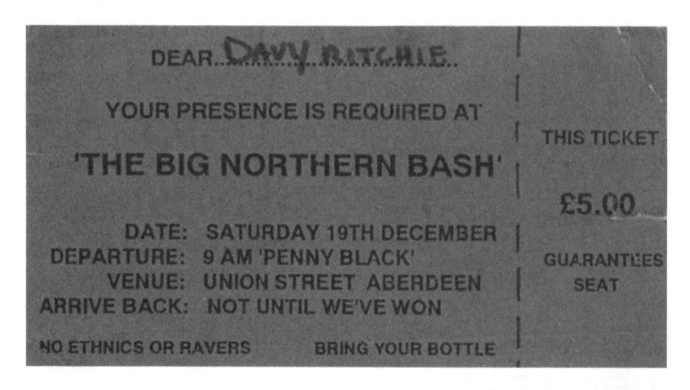

DEAR DAVY RITCHIE

YOUR PRESENCE IS REQUIRED AT

'THE BIG NORTHERN BASH'

DATE: SATURDAY 19TH DECEMBER
DEPARTURE: 9 AM 'PENNY BLACK'
VENUE: UNION STREET ABERDEEN
ARRIVE BACK: NOT UNTIL WE'VE WON

THIS TICKET
£5.00
GUARANTEES SEAT

NO ETHNICS OR RAVERS   BRING YOUR BOTTLE

COMMISERATIONS, YOU HAVE JUST MET THE »CCS«